MW01706051

the 2009 INDISPENSABLE *wine guide*

Also by Joëlle Thomson

The Indispensable Wine Guide, 2005, 2006, 2007, 2008

Celebrating New Zealand Wine, 2004

Joëlle Thomson's Under $20 Wine Guide, 1999, 2000, 2001, 2002, 2003, 2004

101 Wine Tips, 2002

The Global Encyclopedia of Wine, 2000 (co-writer of the New Zealand section)

the 2009 INDISPENSABLE *wine guide*

JOËLLE THOMSON

HarperCollins*Publishers*

National Library of New Zealand Cataloguing-in-Publication Data
Thomson, Joëlle.
The indispensable wine guide 2009 : wines under $25 / Joëlle Thomson.
ISBN 978-1-86950-664-3
1. Wine—Prices—New Zealand—Handbooks, manuals, etc.
2. Wine and wine making—New Zealand—Handbooks, manuals, etc. I. Title.
641.220993—dc 22

First published 2008
HarperCollinsPublishers (New Zealand) Limited
P.O.Box 1, Shortland Street, Auckland

ISBN: 978 1 86950 664 3

Cover design by Matt Stanton
Cover image by Roman Sigaev/Shutterstock.com
Typesetting by IslandBridge

Printed by Griffin Press, Australia.
70gsm Classic used by HarperCollins*Publishers* is a natural, recyclable product made from wood grown in sustainable forests. The manufacturing processes conform to the environmental regulations in the country of origin, Finland.

Contents

Acknowledgements

Thank you to all the winemakers, wine importers and distributors who send their wines in and bring them to my house for tasting. Without such generous and open-minded support, this book, my columns in magazines and newspapers, and my new wine blog (www.mindfood.com) would not exist.

Every time a bottle is sent in, I am charged with the task of honestly appraising its merits – or not. There is no question of rating it kindly just because it's been sent in, sans the cost of purchase. Everything that is sent gets tasted and finds its way onto my own A–Z 'database' of tasting notes or into this book.

Thank you to those who have made writing this book worthwhile – from both the tasting and writing perspective.

Thank you to my publishers at HarperCollins New Zealand.

And finally, thank you to those who make tasting wine as intellectually stimulating as it can be delicious. You know who you are.

About the author

Joëlle Thomson always planned to write about something she loved, but it was only when working as a flambé waitress in the Shetland Islands in Scotland that she decided that 'something' would be wine.

Since graduating from journalism school at Wellington Polytechnic in New Zealand in 1989, Joëlle has worked as a TV copywriter, provincial newspaper journalist and barmaid in New Zealand and the United Kingdom. She penned her first column at the *Capital Times* in Wellington in mid-1994, and has never stopped going to wine tastings since.

Today, Joëlle is the wine editor and associate editor for *MiNDFOOD* magazine, the Auckland correspondent for *New Zealand Winegrower* and *Off Licence News*, and a contributor to other magazines and newspapers. She is a member of the British-based Circle of Wine Writers, and judges wine and food competitions in New Zealand and further afield.

Introduction

Welcome to my eleventh guide to the best wines in New Zealand to suit your budget. It seems like yesterday that a publisher phoned me to talk about writing wine books that would be as easy to read as good wine is to drink. Those are my words, actually, but that phone call was a meeting of the minds – and tastebuds.

Since the first incarnation of this book in 1999, it has grown from an under-$15 wine guide to an under-$20 wine guide to this *Indispensable Wine Guide*, which includes ratings and tastings and a guide to all wines available in New Zealand under $25.

The book is not about numbers. Nor should your drinking be. A good glass of wine is not about size, cost or even alcohol content. It is about taste. This is why the 'drink less, drink better' mantra only works when you've got some of that better wine on hand. That's where this book comes in. Every single wine in the guide has been re-tasted, re-rated and re-written about this year.

The aim is to deliver you the very best wines, so read through, check out the highest-rating wines in your favourite categories and, first and foremost, take a risk on a good-looking, high-rating wine and enjoy.

Salut!
Joëlle

Wine faults

Wine faults exist in wines of all prices, but most are easy to spot if you're armed with a little knowledge. The following guide should help point you in the right direction, and empower you to steer yourself away from the wrong wines.

If you think cork taint sounds difficult to get your head around, then here's another wine fault for you: brettanomyces, volatile acidity and mercaptans. Actually, that's three.

The point is that wine faults come in various shapes and sizes and are the single biggest cause of disagreement between winemakers, wine writers and other judges at wine competitions all over the world. And in a world where screwcaps are becoming ever more significant, many wine faults are becoming ever more obvious – sticking out like sore thumbs, you could say.

There are a number of simple wine faults that are relatively easy to identify once they have been pointed out, explained and tasted. And most winemakers and wine distributors are able to assist wine waiting staff to identify these faults.

The number of times that I have had to practically beg bar staff to open another bottle because a glass of wine I'm drinking from one already opened is in poor condition is . . . well, far too often.

While I am confident about the particular tastes of corked, oxidised, volatile and brettanomyces-infected wines, most wine drinkers are not. But one thing that everybody who consumes wine can taste is whether or not they like a wine.

If a bottle tastes wrong, send it back. You don't have to know the lingo to have the confidence to articulate that you're not happy with the taste of a wine. Ask for a new glass from a fresh bottle, or take it back to where you purchased it and ask for another bottle – it helps your case no end, obviously, if you haven't consumed the entire contents and are taking back an empty bottle.

But it's not so much a case of trying to find fault for the sake of it; rather of being informed about some of the faults that can occur in wines.

Oxidation

Oxidised wine is not only that yellow-coloured plonk you once drank, didn't much enjoy and later realised was oxidised wine. Oxidation is insidious and can taste like anything from brown apples to flat or 'dirty' wine. While you can purchase bottles of closed wine that turn out to be oxidised, the most common place you will encounter oxidised wine is when it is served to you in a bar or restaurant because a bottle of wine has been open too long. If you think a glass of wine poured to you while you're out in a bar or restaurant has a flat, plain flavour, ask for a new glass from a newly opened bottle.

Bad wine service

This is, obviously, the opposite of good wine service. And despite the prevalence of overbearing water-jug waiters, good service is about far more than the continuous topping up of your wine and water glasses. Anyone who's ever had a corked or oxidised wine served to them, either by the glass or by the bottle, knows what I'm talking about. It is up to those serving wine to understand what corked and oxidised wine tastes like, and if they don't know, they should adhere to that old chestnut about the customer always being right.

Brettanomyces

Okay, so you haven't heard of the wine fault that those in the know refer to colloquially as 'brett', but it is a growing problem, so read on and get to know what you're looking for. It could save you from a lot of disappointing wine-drinking experiences.

Brettanomyces is a strain of yeast that can flatten the flavour to the wines it infects. It can have a 'band-aid' or mousy aroma or flavour, if present at high levels in wine. If you detect flavours such as these that you think overwhelm a wine, it may have 'brett'. Expect to hear a lot more about 'brett' before this decade is out.

Snobbery

Definitely a fault . . . of some wine drinkers, that is. Snobbery is boring and far too pervasive where wine is concerned, because a couple of sips can bring out the worst in those who want to look well rounded in their appreciation of wine. Don't bang on about oak if you don't understand at least a little about how too much oak can absolutely destroy the taste of wine – and why. Better to stick with what you know – 'I like this wine a lot' or 'I'm not enjoying this over-worked chardonnay'. Forget the jargon, unless you can fully participate. It's not impressive.

Cork taint and reduction

It would be churlish to talk about cork taint without mentioning reductivity, which takes different forms but is best described as a rubbery smell and taste. And while cork taint can only occur in wines sealed with corks (of which only about 10 per cent of Kiwi wines now are, due to the move to screwcaps), reduction is now most commonly a by-product of some wines sealed by screwcaps. Reduction occurs most commonly in air-tight environments, which means that screwcaps can be the perfect place for it to develop, as are wines sealed with properly-fitting corks. Decanting wine for a few hours before you drink it can get rid of reductive aromas and flavours. Cork taint cannot be got rid of; if a wine is corked, it is ruined.

Carbon neutral –
what it means for wineries

Whether it's green, red or pink, chances are the wine in the glass you're holding right now is far more environmentally friendly than it was five years ago.

Until the mid-1990s, organic certification in New Zealand was made solely by BioGro, whose rules and regulations were traditionally better suited to horticulture than to viticulture. But now that reducing your carbon footprint has become the hottest thing to do, Kiwi wineries are getting serious about being green.

Late last year the New Zealand wine industry adopted a sustainability policy that will see all of this country's grapes and wine produced under independently audited sustainability schemes by 2012. It is as radical as it sounds.

Since the goal was put in place in 2007, there has been a rapid rise in membership of Sustainable Winegrowing New Zealand (SWNZ), the body that monitors the reduction in the use of pesticides, herbicides and other pollutants used in wine production. Only 71 of the 565 wineries in New Zealand are currently members, but they represent 70 per cent of all Kiwi wine; 70 per cent of the country's vineyards also belong. Membership means that these growers and winemakers are moving towards organic or biodynamic certification by 2012. And if they're not? They won't be able to cash in on that all-important sales tool – marketing.

New Zealand wineries and vineyards need to be members of New Zealand Winegrowers, the official industry body, in order to benefit from the international marketing that the association organises. 'We can't make them belong, but if they don't, our stipulation is that they will not be part of any of the annual joint marketing initiatives that we undertake, which is one of our main roles,' explains New Zealand Winegrowers chief executive officer, Philip Gregan.

'And while we can't assist with costs to every one of nearly 600 wineries, we are making sure that we minimise the costs for small vineyards and wineries going down this path. We can't subsidise them, because at the end of the day, the biggest cost is being independently audited and that's what has to happen.'

Last year, a New Zealand winery won the first-ever Planet Earth Sustainability Trophy at the world's biggest wine competition, the London-based International Wine Challenge. Over 9000 wines from around the world were entered, and Bald Hills Vineyard from Central Otago won the award for its Bald Hills Pinot Noir 2005. 'Our sustainability was driven from the vineyard where three years ago we introduced inter-row cultivation and a cover crop programme, from which we have grown a bulk green crop and turned this back into the soil . . . which has enabled improved organic matter, water withholding capacity and general soil structure,' says Dr Blair Hunt, co-owner of the Bald Hills winery with his wife, Estelle.

The catch-cry at Amisfield Winery in Central Otago is similar. 'We lease our land from our grandchildren, and we want this farm to be in a better condition when we shuffle off this mortal coil than when we took it on,' says Amisfield winemaker Jeff Sinnott.

When the second Amisfield winery opened at Lowburn in 2006, a wetland was installed. 'The idea came from an old irrigation dam we had on the land, which is topped up from a stream that runs out of a mountain. We could see there was a range of species that survived in both the extremes of winter and summer, so we thought native species that adapted to this environment would help to ameloriate wastewater,' Sinnott explains. 'In Central Otago water is a fairly scarce commodity, so the idea of preserving and maintaining this precious resource is to make sure that the outputs from the winery were as neutral as possible,' he adds.

How toxic is winery wastewater? 'Wineries do not use a lot of chemicals. In the bad old days we used chlorine and caustic soda, but these days we're using soft cleaning agents, such as citric acid. We've put the Janola bottle back on the shelf and we've picked up a bottle of vinegar, so to speak. These days we use steam, hot water and ozone to clean things out. And if we have to sterilise everything we use peroxide (H_2O_2),' Sinnott says.

These treatments break down in water, and the wetland doubles as a bio-indicator of winery waste and a home for native birds, such as paradise ducks and guinea fowl, and frogs.

New Zealand's first carbon-zero winery is Grove Mill, which is aiming to make its home vineyard organically certified with BioGro New Zealand. The winery was carbon-zero accredited in September 2006.

Sustainable development manager, Roger Kerrison, says Grove Mill became carbon-zero accredited by becoming part of Landcare Research's CarboNZero programme. 'We purchase carbon credits from an accredited programme that Landcare Research is running. A credit is the equivalent of one tonne of carbon dioxide, measured via the Kyoto Protocol. The credits that Grove Mill is purchasing are all farm based.'

Land that is marginal for farming is allowed to seed into native bush, which is then put into trust, and the farmer gets the equivalent of CO_2 that the bush stores to sell as carbon credits.

And then there are biodynamics, in which a farm, vineyard or garden is treated as a holistic, self-contained entity. Demeter International is the official certification organisation for biodynamic agriculture. Biodynamics was founded by the Austrian philosopher, the late Rudolph Steiner.

Fault lines

In 2007, Master of Wine Sam Harrop spearheaded the biggest investigation into wine faults ever undertaken, at the 2007 International Wine Challenge (IWC) held in London, when he and the other judges broadened their focus on wine faults.

The aim of the research was to share its findings with the wine industry to help guide further technical research to influence industry practices in an effort to improve wine quality, Harrop explained. It was ambitious, he conceded, trying to analyse every single faulty wine and record the results to the extent they did at the previous year's IWC. But by streamlining the general judging process, they improved the reliability of awards and had more time to give wine faults the attention they deserved.

'Every time a judging panel sent through a faulty wine, I tasted it again to validate the judging panel's conclusion and to verify the nature of the fault and ascertain whether the flavours were excessive enough to be deemed a fault point blank,' says Harrop.

To get fair results in a sensory study such as this, it was important to take a conservative approach to recording faults, not least because individual thresholds vary greatly between tasters, and there are differing opinions as to what constitutes a fault. 'Obviously, cork taint is clear cut, in that if it is present at any detectable level, it is deemed a fault and another bottle is opened,' Harrop says.

By contrast, other faults are not so simple to categorise – sulphides, volatile phenols and volatile acidity, to name but a few. 'The subjectivity here is for the most part about whether the levels of these compounds are excessive or not. Some wine competitions might consider any evidence of sulphides or volatile phenols to be faulty, but the IWC takes a more open-minded approach, recognising that complexity and balance are key concepts in defining wine quality,' says Harrop.

'Certain levels of certain sulphides and volatile phenols can add to the complexity of the wine. Where the flavours become excessive, the wine quality is impaired and the wine is deemed faulty. If there is a question mark over whether a wine is faulty once it gets to my table, I put it back into circulation for rejudging by another panel, following the logic that four palates are better than one,' he adds.

Despite misreporting on sulphidic characters under screwcaps which found its way to the media earlier this year, a direct comparison between levels of sulphidic characters under screwcaps versus sulphidic characters under cork was not made in last year's IWC faults analysis. The notion that wines sealed with screwcaps had higher levels of sulphides than their cork-sealed counterparts was, therefore, conjecture only.

Rather than leave it that way, Harrop intends to find out the facts behind the faults, extending the scope of analysis at this year's IWC to look at comparable excess sulphide rates under screwcaps and those under corks. This way the trade will be in a position to compare sulphide rates between the two closures. 'This should provide interesting reading for winemakers looking to package wines with maximum fruit intensity to meet the export markets' demands,' Harrop says.

All wines went through rigorous sensory faults analysis and any deemed even vaguely faulty went through at least two rounds of appraisal before being registered as having legitimate faults. But this was no witch hunt. Like any winemaker keen on any aspect of winemaking, Harrop's motivation for pushing boundaries in faults analysis at this competition is to provide information to winemakers around the world to help them improve wine quality for the consumer.

'We're not suggesting that our analysis is 100 per cent foolproof, because this is sensory rather than laboratory analysis, but to do it chemically it would take for ever and cost tens of thousands of pounds, so we are putting the best controls in place that we can,' he says.

Closure-related faults were still the most serious fault issue for the trade, ranging from TCA (2,4,6-trichloroanisole) and reduction to oxidation. 'Putting TCA to one side, it is clear from last year's IWC results that reduction is a bigger issue than oxidation, primarily because, in a general sense, over the years winemakers have moved from an oxidative process to a more reductive one in their search for fruit,' Harrop says.

Of all the countries that entered wines into the 2006 IWC, New Zealand had the lowest incidence of sulphide faults, which Harrop attributes to greater experience with the screwcap closure. Incidentally, New Zealand also had the highest usage of screwcaps per entry into the 2006 IWC. 'This is clear evidence that New Zealand has a much better grasp on this technical closure than other producing nations,' he says.

'Wine faults arise through a number of different avenues, including fruit quality, poor fermentation management, bottling unstable product, making inappropriate decisions when it comes to packaging, and perhaps most importantly when it comes to the screwcap issue, inadequate preparation of the wine before bottling.

'I get sick to death of seeing these articles suggesting that screwcaps have a direct link to a sulphide character. If a wine sealed with a screwcap shows excessive levels of sulphide, then it's the winemaker's fault, not the closure's fault. Screwcaps are a technical closure and for the most part deliver what their salespeople promise

– a reductive and effective seal for a consistent and fresher flavour in the glass. Manufacturers let themselves down not on the factory floor itself, but in their inability to educate winemakers on the technical practices necessary to optimise wine quality.'

Since writing his Master of Wine dissertation on 'The Role of Brettanomyces in the Production of High-quality Syrah-based Wines' in 2003, Harrop concedes he has gained a reputation for having a slightly 'unhealthy' level of interest in wine faults. 'My aim is to try and educate people about the importance of understanding how to manage fault levels to give the consumer better value,' he asserts. 'What other industry has a customer base that accepts a fault rate of over seven per cent? Wine consumers deserve a better deal. The IWC faults work is about giving winemakers more information to improve wine quality and consistency for their customers.'

Misreporting in many newspapers around the world held that the IWC found faulty wines under screwcap, but this was a misrepresentation of the facts. 'This was frustrating, given the huge amount of work that went into this research. I'm bewildered why certain commentators just focused on screwcaps and didn't pick up on some of the other arguably more important findings reported,' Harrop says.

Other such findings include that 2.19 per cent of all red wines tasted were considered to have excessive levels of volatile phenols, presumably from brettanomyces activity.

Nearly 50 per cent of the wine faults detected at the 2006 IWC were related to the type of closure, but few journalists have yet written about the fact that the natural cork fault rate was more than twice that of the screwcap sulphide fault rate, adds Harrop. 'Nor has there been much written about oxidation arising from poor natural cork quality as observed in 1.6 per cent of all wines bottled with the cork. If you consider how many more wines are bottled with cork than with screwcaps around the world, then 1.6 per cent is hugely significant.

'The 2006 IWC showed that cork companies might well have succeeded in getting cork taint down to 2.8 per cent, but at what expense? Perhaps they have taken their eye off some critical control points in the manufacturing process, which might result in dryer and less elastic corks in the bottle that will lead to oxidation,' he says.

And, yes, there is an opportunity for taint-free corks (such as Diam) and screwcaps to live in symbiosis, reckons Harrop. 'Diam is a good cork; it can enhance reductivity but it's taint free. And for screwcap fans to fight against Diam or cork is silly, I think. They should just celebrate the success they've both had and get on with their business of selling more closures.'

Little is understood about what gives some people a higher or lower sensory threshold for other wine faults, such as brettanomyces, but it is clear that one wine-lover's smelly, intolerably dirty barnyard flavour is another's slightly dirty, interestingly dodgy activity (yes, we're still talking about wine here).

Anyone whose palate has yet to tell them that barking up the brettanomyces tree is a bunch of old rot only needs to read Harrop's dissertation to understand that excessive levels of the by-products of brettanomyces can render wine aromas and flavours technically flat, dull and volatile.

On the other hand, 'a certain level just above the threshold can win you a lot of admirers,' Harrop says. 'The reason I chose syrah as the subject was because quite often I thought that Northern Rhône syrahs had a "bretty" character when quite often it was actually a complex sulphide flavour aroma; often the flavour expression of certain sulphides is quite similar to the volatile phenols produced by "brett" which makes things quite complex when reviewing faults. I wanted to try and demystify that syrah is no more susceptible to brettanomyces than any other full-bodied red variety.'

His paper explains that phenolic acids in wines are a precursor to brettanomyces activity, so the more grape skins and seeds that are extracted, the greater the concentration of these precursors. 'In short, if you're into high levels of extraction in your winemaking, you have a greater risk of getting uncontrolled brettanomyces activity,' Harrop says.

Not that he enthuses only about pristine and clean-tasting wines. 'The best wines, I think, sit in the middle of the classic styles we think of as being typical of the New World and the Old World,' he says. 'The best wines have a detectable but balanced level of some of these compounds responsible for faulty wines, such as volatile acidity, volatile phenols and various types of sulphides. The key point is being able to appraise quality – if you don't know what certain key faults are, how can you judge what quality is?'

Wine competitions

Few wine competitions have such a focus on wine faults, but the quality of judging – and of the wines themselves – has risen massively in this country in the last few decades. In the 'old days', which is how Royal Easter Wine Show director Terry Dunleavy refers to the 1970s, a bronze medal was a sign that a wine didn't have any obvious faults. It may not have had much merit either, adds Dunleavy.

The overall improvement in the quality of New Zealand wines means that it is more difficult now than it was back then to get a gold, silver or bronze medal. And a bronze medal awarded at the Royal Easter Wine Show in its 54th year now means that a wine has positive qualities – as you would hope.

Also worth noting is that judges at the 2007 Royal Easter Show Wine Awards dished out fewer gold and bronze medals this year than last. Despite receiving more wines in for judging, only 76 golds were awarded this year compared with 79 last year; bronzes totalled 502, down from 507 last year.

It might not sound like a lot, but it reflects the fact that medals are not given out simply for the sake of it.

Wine cellars

Wine cellars are often made up of a motley mixture of great wines, quirky finds and complete duds. Until they are opened, even the great wines are an unknown quantity, although well-chosen wines do evolve into even more delicious creatures than when first purchased. The others are usually a mixture of the good, the bad and the downright undrinkable. This is because most people collect wine that they have chosen according to what they enjoy drinking now, without always thinking about how that wine might taste in the future.

The simple fact is that most wines nowadays are made with the intention of being consumed within a few hours of purchase, so it's important you have some to consume on hand.

Wines that do not age well and should not be cellared:

- Boxed wines or 'cask' wines.
- Pink and rosé wines.
- Sweet sparkling wines.
- Most wines made from hybrid and crossed grapes such as anything made from albany surprise, breidecker and white diamond, among a host of other curiosities made for drinking young.

Wines that do age well and should be cellared:

- Burgundy: red and white (medium term).
- Cabernet sauvignon: those from top wineries in Australia,

Bordeaux, the western USA (California), Chile and some other places and producers (with the occasional New Zealand one worth keeping – such as Coleraine).

- Châteauneuf-du-Pape: medium to long term, depending on the year and the producer.
- Barolo: Italy's greatest wine.
- Riesling: from Alsace, France; the Clare and Eden Valleys in Australia; and the Rhine and Mosel regions in Germany (medium to long term, and particularly long term in the case of most German wines).
- Shiraz and syrah: medium to long term, depending always on the producer, the year and the wine region. The best come from the Rhône Valley, France and from Australia.

Remember, only wines that taste great to start off with get better with time.

When you start collecting wine . . .

Two bottles of each wine is the minimum that you need in order to start a serious collection. This is so that you have an extra bottle in case you suspect that the other is corked or oxidised. If both bottles are fine, the second one provides you with the possibility of revisiting its flavours another year, if you have the willpower to keep it that long.

Keeping wine to see how the flavours and style change over time is the whole point of having a wine cellar, so it's preferable to buy more than two bottles if you can.

Screwcaps

A screw loose

You may not realise it, but a quiet revolution has been happening in the wine industry right under your nose. That familiar sound of the popping cork is being silenced by the gentle twist of the screwcap.

Corks are on death row, and while debate still rages on, red wines will age and evolve positively in the long term under screwcaps. For light, young, soft red wines, screwcaps are just the ticket.

If 2004 was a watershed for screwcaps, which still constitute the biggest positive change for wine in the world this millennium, then last year was yet another moment of truth for wine seals. This year 90 per cent of New Zealand wine is sealed with screwcaps, and that figure is predicted to rise to 95 per cent by the time all of the wines from the 2007 vintage have been bottled.

There are issues sometimes with red wines under screwcaps and there is the very occasional screwcap that is difficult to get off a bottle, but both of these issues can be dealt with and pale in comparison with the number of broken corks, oxidised and corked wines that I experience and the nasty little cuts I get all over my hands when I'm trying to open the foil that is placed over the tops of many corks.

Call me clumsy (cutting myself on a corkscrew and wine foil), but dealing with corks is all too hard now that screwcaps have made wine more accessible and easier. No wonder Kiwis are drinking more wine – it's easier to open than it's ever been before now that screwcaps are here to stay.

Screwcaps are so easy to open that I sometimes forget they

were revived to eliminate cork taint. And while they are not perfect – reductive rubbery smells can be an issue in some wines, and on one occasion a cap simply would not come off – screwcaps are brilliant for ease of use, chucking away the corkscrew (nearly) and keeping wine fresh.

Screwcaps have also removed some of the snobbery inherent in wine. The biggest reason I love them is that screwcaps have made the world of difference to the taste of white wines, which are fresher and cleaner than ever. Oh, and in the four-and-a-half years that screwcaps have been used, during which time one screwcap that I experienced stuck like cement on a bottle, I have lost count of the number of broken corks, corked and oxidised wines that I have experienced during the same period.

Screwed or corked?

It is the most contentious issue in wine circles right now – to screw it shut, or to stuff a bit of old tree bark in the top of a bottle. That is what cork is – remarkable, unique and unrivalled by any other natural or synthetic product, but still a bit of tree bark from the heat-loving cork oak, which is grown mostly in the hottest parts of Spain, Portugal and northern Africa.

Here are a few of the pertinent facts and figures:

Corks

- Are directly responsible for randomly causing oxidation and cork taint (*not* bits of cork floating in a bottle, but an off-odour and taste that occurs at varying levels in wine).
- Have always been known to cause these problems, but because they do so randomly and so variably, it is impossible to put a percentage figure on how many bottles are affected.
- Give off their own woody taste even when they do not allow excess air into the wine or impart an off-taste.

Screwcaps

- Are an almost hermetic (air-tight) seal, and trials over decades by the Australian Wine Research Institute show them to be a far more reliable stopper for wines.
- Do allow white wines to taste more consistent, meaning the out-moded saying 'there are no great wines, only great bottles' applies only to those bottles sealed with a cork. If a wine is good under a screwcap, then every bottle will taste good.
- Are most preferable on fresh, aromatic white wines that have such light fruity flavours that cork influence is immediately detectable (once you are used to the alternative) – wines such as gewürztraminer, riesling, pinot gris and sauvignon blanc are particularly good under screwcap.

While the debate rages, most New Zealand winemakers are now on the side of the screwcap because, in comparative tastings, wines sealed this way always taste fresher – unless the screwcap is damaged.

It's not just New Zealand wines that are growing in screwcap usage. The world's most famous and influential wine writer, north American Robert Parker, estimates that by the year 2015, about 95 per cent of the world's wines will be sealed with screwcaps. Which brings up the very serious issue of what Portugal will do with all those cork oak trees. Who knows? Cork tiles may have a renaissance.

For now there is no compelling evidence to suggest that red wines are better under screwcaps, save for anecdotal tastings, but research is underway both here and overseas on this.

The screwcap versus cork debate is enormous and complex. Find out more at www.screwcap.co.nz

Crowning glory

Screwcaps are not being used to seal bottles of bubbles, but there is a way forward from cork which impacts as much on bubbles as it does on any other liquid product it is used to seal (and, yes, I have had several bottles of bubbles that have been 'corked', just as I have tasted corked whisky and corked olive oil).

The way forward for bubbles is the crown seal, also known as a crown cap and used most commonly on bottles of beer. Crown seals are used on bubbles that are produced via the traditional method – hence the appellation 'méthode traditionelle' – where they undergo their secondary fermentation in the bottle prior to disgorgement (unsealing and bottling). Champagne is at the top of the tree, but any wine with bubbles can also be made this way.

And as for that old chestnut about the romance and the pop of the cork, it is completely misguided. As French winemakers always say, and Christian Pol-Roger is particularly fond of wheeling out: 'You don't want a bottle of champagne ever to pop, you want it to sigh – like the sigh of a contented woman.'

Earlier this millennium, Dr Tony Jordan, head winemaker at Domaine Chandon, based in Australia's Yarra Valley and owned by Moët & Chandon (the world's biggest champagne producer), bravely sealed one of the winery's top bubbles with a crown seal. It was an audacious move in an industry within an industry – high-quality fizz – that is obsessed with tradition.

The wine that Jordan sealed with the crown seals was not the everyday Chandon bubbly, but a new sparkling wine called Chandon Z*D – a bone-dry 'zero dosage' bubbly – made from grapes grown in the Yarra Valley and due to be launched here in October this year.

As to what the head honchos at the parent company thought of one of their products under a crown seal, Jordan's body language immediately says it all as he folds his arms, forces a smile and confesses he did not want to create a stir but knew he had to do something about the insidious problem of corked bubbly.

The pros and cons of his provocative move were discussed at length between Jordan and his bosses in France. He won. And the company has subsequently designed and manufactured its own wine key, which is used widely and increasingly in Sydney restaurants. The key not only unlocks the crown seal but does so with as much aplomb as anyone could ever use to gently ease a cork out of a bottle.

Glassware

Riedel and Riedel O

To describe Austrian glass company Riedel as the pre-eminent wineglass manufacturer in the world is an understatement. Begun in 1673 by Johann Christoph Riedel, this Bohemian glass merchant is today run by Georg Riedel and his son Maximillian. Their newest innovations are the Tyrol glass range – stemless lead-crystal glasses on a stylish wedge base – and the 'O' series of stemless glasses, designed to enhance the aroma and taste of specific wine types. Riedel glassware is available at Glengarry liquor stores in the North Island and at good specialist kitchen stores nationwide. Find out more from the importer, Hancocks, phone (09) 379 3740.

Spiegelau

It may not have the warm-fuzzy family-owned story of Riedel, but Spiegelau glassware is every bit as good when it comes to the taste of your wine. Their extensive range comes in many different shapes and sizes – there is even a specially designed glass from which to drink zinfandel. Spiegelau glassware is available at selected specialist wine stores nationwide.

Eisch Breathable

It is difficult to believe that glassware can 'breathe', but the makers of this range are sure that it can. Their crystal has undergone a proprietary treatment that allows the wine to aerate a few minutes after it has been poured, improving the taste of the wine.

Eisch Breathable glassware is available via importers Bennett & Deller Wine Merchants; for stockists, phone (09) 378 9463.

Glossary

The following guide to wine words is intended to assist, inform and amuse readers (the latter is the easiest task of these, given that wine writing is laden with unusual, inadequate and, far too often, inappropriately pompous-sounding adjectives).

Flavour is extremely difficult to describe – as any wine or food writer will tell you and as radio reviewer David Hill wrote in *The Listener* on 4 October 2003 when he took great joy in quoting a radio music critic: ' "Harmonically audacious . . . turbulent and uneasy . . . serious and intense": is this where wine writers get their adjectives?' asked Hill. The difference, he opined, between wine writers and those on the radio programme he was describing was that the latter used such adjectives thoughtfully. He had a point.

It is too easy to use jargon that has resonance within the wine biz and overlook the rest of the world where nobody understands what an audacious, turbulent or intense-tasting wine actually tastes like. Having never used words such as 'harmonically audacious', 'turbulent' and 'uneasy' to describe a wine, I can only guess at what those who have used them actually mean.

The most thoughtful writers try to give wine jargon the swerve, but even they simply do need to use some of the following words every now and then.

Clean

Self-explanatory term meaning that a wine is and tastes technically clean, i.e. it is devoid of faults and taints from either the vineyard, winery or the way the wine is sealed.

Complex

A subjective wine word meaning there is more to this wine than meets the mouth in the first sip. It is not one-dimensional but rather multi-layered or multi-faceted, and has what many wine jargon users might describe as 'layers of flavours'.

Fruit-driven

One of the most over-used phrases in the wine lexicon and a hallmark of most New Zealand sauvignon blancs and Australian shirazes, in which fruit flavours are usually overtly pronounced.

Intense

Used to mean oomph, body, weight and guts. An intense wine is one with lots going for it – not light, thin or pale, in other words.

Multi-layered

Another way of saying that a wine is 'complex' (see above) and has lots of different flavours. A multi-layered wine could also be described as an interesting wine.

Oaked

A wine which has been treated to some time in oak, either during fermentation or afterwards. Chardonnay is the most commonly oaked white wine, while most reds spend some of their lives, pre-bottling, in oak or surrounded by it (many cheap wines usually see oak in the form of tea-bag-like oak chips or an oak stave plonked into a stainless steel tank to impart flavour).

Serious

Hideously over-used word in the wine world – and the world in general; used to confer the notion of something very good.

Unoaked

Usually used in relation to chardonnays, often to convey the stylistic difference between a lighter chardonnay style (unoaked) compared with a weightier, more usual chardonnay style. Most chardonnays are at least partially oaked, meaning that a component of the finished wine usually sees some oak.

Vintage

Surprisingly often misused word meaning, simply, the year in which the grapes were grown from which the wine was made.

Author's predictions

- Experiencing better wine service in bars, cafés and restaurants, which will eventually occur due to the launch in New Zealand of the Master Sommelier qualification in both on-premise (restaurants) and off-premise (liquor stores and supermarkets) outlets. The country's largest wine company, Pernod Ricard New Zealand, is at the helm of launching and steering this new qualification in the right directions in New Zealand.
- Better wine glasses in bars, cafés and restaurants. They don't have to be Riedel or Spiegelau (although I'll love it if you go that way), but there does need to be a revamp of most of the dire glassware that wine is served in.
- Less moral panic about drinking a glass of wine a day or every few days. We know a little alcohol is better for you than none at all. It's time New Zealanders learnt moderation in their thinking as well as their drinking, and stopped apologising for their new-found passion for a little bit of what they fancy . . .
- Tasting more Waipara rieslings without price tags that break the bank. Love the taste, austerity, dryness and style of the wines from this growing Cantabrian region.
- More screwcaps used on wines made here, which mostly means white wines made to drink when they are relatively young. This means more consistency of style and clean, fresh wines.
- Spain's continued rise in our minds and mouths as more great-

value and good-tasting reds (plus a smattering of whites) pour into New Zealand.

- Argentinian reds increasing in quality and quantity too, and not just gutsy wines made from malbec, but a wider range of high-quality, though not highly priced, wines.

- The continued ascendancy of good gin and tonic (with lime only, thank you) now that the world is finally realising vodka is the pinot gris of the spirit world.

- And hopefully some better pinot gris and more consistency in the style of this obviously challenging grape, so that the wines we taste labelled 'pinot gris' begin to have just a smidgeon of consistency.

While I am now less optimistic about moral panic, which seems to rise like a tsunami in this country where alcohol is concerned – with some good reason but often misdirected worries – there are good things that have happened over the last year on this country's wine scene:

- Pinot gris has got better at mid to high price points.
- Spanish wine continues to grow in quality and the number available in New Zealand.
- Argentinian malbec continues to grow in quality and availability globally and in this country.

My wish list for the next year

Better wine service in this country from cafés and bars to restaurants, which would consist of:

- Continued rise in use of top-quality glassware in bars and restaurants – this is definitely taking place.

- A far broader range of wines available by the glass and bottle – i.e. more experimentation by those choosing the wines. You don't have to commit to a year's supply of a new wine to make an interesting list; just buy a few cases and blackboard the wine by the glass as a special trial.
- Less argumentative wait staff when it comes to consumer complaints about corked and oxidised wine. If you don't know, then at least be polite to the customer and be willing to open another bottle. You can either get a credit on the first bottle if it is faulty, or you can serve it to less tricky customers if it's not faulty.
- More experimental restaurateurs – it's not the wait staff's fault if the wine list is as boring as . . . well, let's just say it's up to the owner most of the time to be open-minded about new wine styles from further afield than just our own backyard.
- Less moral panic about drinking. Okay, so we're drinking more alcohol generally than we were a decade ago, but we are only consuming about a teaspoon or two more of wine per day than we were a couple of years ago. Let's put this is in perspective: Kiwis, on average, consumed 3.2 litres more alcohol in 2005 than they did in 2004, and local wine consumption was up, but beer still constitutes 68 per cent of alcohol consumed in this country, while wine only makes up 6.8 per cent.

Wines of the year

First, a question: should I choose a wine of the year that I know will be a one-glass wonder with most wine drinkers? Or should I choose a wine of the year that I honestly think is the very best wine under $25 in New Zealand? It's more difficult to answer than you might think.

If I choose the former, then wine drinkers both inside and outside the wine industry will say something along the lines of 'Ah, that Joëlle; she has found the juiciest, most delicious wine around for the budget price wine guide' . . . and then after a glass or two, they will tire of the big juicy wine I have chosen as wine of the year.

If I choose the wine that I genuinely think is the very best of all those submitted to this guide, then you might not immediately think 'Wow! What a zingy, orgasmic wine!' but after a couple of sips, you will be wowed. And after two glasses you'll realise that one bottle just isn't enough . . .

At the beginning and end of the day, I have to live with the choices I make, which means I have chosen the wine I think has the best balance and most character of all sent in to this guide.

The quest for the best wine available in New Zealand under $25 is no easy task. And just because this is the eleventh budget wine guide I have written does not mean it gets any easier. To begin with, there are the invites to send out to wineries and wine importers and distributors, asking them to submit the wines they want to be included in this guide. Then there are the follow-ups . . . and the next follow-ups.

And then there are all the boxes that arrive on my doorstep

and need to be unwrapped and disposed of, and finally there is the sheer quantity of wine to be tasted to come up with the best wine.

Add to that the notion of laying subjectivity to one side, and you have an almost impossible task – one that is akin to asking somebody who doesn't wear perfume to rate the most attractive aromas in a long line-up of perfume.

Happy drinking!

Wine of the year

2006 Armantes Old Bush Vine Garnacha

$17–$19 ☆☆☆☆½

This is a great wine. Dark in colour, richly fruity in taste but bone dry, it tastes delicious now and history shows that it ages well too, provided you're keeping it in a cool, dark spot. Armantes is a range of mountains in Spain, where 50-year-old garnacha (aka Grenache) grapes are grown at a high altitude. Master of Wine Steve Bennett and Matt Deller import it to New Zealand, introducing Kiwis to a world of other wine flavours. Needless to say, it is great value – and I chose it as my wine of the year for its wide appeal to all wine drinkers.

Specialist wine stores or contact Bennett & Deller for stockists near you, phone (09) 378 9463

Star wines of the year

Star chardonnay

2006 Lonestone Hawke's Bay Chardonnay $20 ☆☆☆☆

Star gewürztraminer

2007 Montana Riverpoint Gisborne Matawhero Gewürztraminer $24–25 ☆☆☆½

Star pinot gris

2007 Clayridge Marlborough Pinot Gris $24–25 ☆☆☆☆

Star riesling

2006 Knappstein Clare Valley Hand Picked Riesling
$22–24 ☆☆☆☆½

Star sauvignon blanc

2007 Mahi Marlborough Sauvignon Blanc $19–20 ☆☆☆☆½

Star semillon

2006 Jacob's Creek Semillon Chardonnay $10–12 ☆☆☆

Star soave

2006 Pasqua Soave Classico $15–16 ☆☆☆½

Star viognier

2007 Villa Maria Cellar Selection Hawke's Bay Viognier
$24–25 ☆☆☆☆

Star rosé

2006 Clayridge Marlborough Pinot Rosé $22–23 ☆☆☆☆

Star cabernet

2005 Sandalford Protégé Cabernet Merlot Margaret River
$20–21 ☆☆☆☆

Star chianti

2007 Piccini Chianti $16–18 ☆☆☆½

Star Côtes-du-Rhône

2005 M Chapoutier Côtes-du-Rhône Belleruche
$20–21 ☆☆☆½

Star malbec

2005 Trapiche Broquel Malbec $19–20 ☆☆☆½

Star merlot

2006 Preece Merlot $18–20 ☆☆☆☆

Star montepulciano

2007 Valle Reale Vigne Nuove Montepulciano $22–23 ☆☆☆☆

Star negroamaro

2006 Menhir NZero Negroamaro $20 ☆☆☆½

Star nero d'avolas – double winners

2006 Corallo Nero d'Avola Sicilia $10–12 ☆☆☆☆

2006 La Mura Nero d'Avola $14–15 ☆☆☆☆

Star other Italian red

2007 Tegole Piccini Toscana IGT $16–18 ☆☆☆☆

Star pinot noir

2006 Montana Reserve Pinot Noir $24–25 ☆☆☆½

Star primitivo

2004 Canaletto Primitivo $19–20 ☆☆☆☆

Star sangiovese

2006 Cecchi Bonizio Sangiovese di Maremma $19–20 ☆☆☆½

Star shiraz

2005 Grant Burge Barossa Vines Shiraz $19–20 ☆☆☆☆½

Star valpolicella

2006 Bolla Valpolicella Classico $18–19 ☆☆☆½

Star bubbly

Lindauer Special Reserve 2004 $24–25 ☆☆☆☆

Star bubbly under $10

Bernadino Spumante $8–9 ☆☆☆½

Star prosecco

Bolla Prosecco NV $22–23 ☆☆☆☆

Star dessert wine

2006 Gran Feudo Blanco Dulce de Moscatel $24–25 ☆☆☆☆½

Star fortified wine

Orlando Liqueur Port $18–20 ☆☆☆½

Star sherry

Sandeman Dry Sec Sherry $18–20 ☆☆☆½

White wines

Blanc de noir

'Blonk de nwa'

To describe 'blanc de noir' as being as rare as hen's teeth is to wildly understate the obvious. Analyse the name and you'll quickly discover that this wine is, indeed, 'white from red' – a white wine made from red grapes. In the case of the one wine in this chapter, the red grapes were solely pinot noir. Hand-picked, kept free of skin contact (in order to minimise colour pick-up) and then kept cool during fermentation, this wine has surprising weight.

2007 Richmond Plains Nelson Blanc de Noir $18–20

☆☆☆☆ Screwcap

Pink in colour, weighty in body and fresh in taste, this surprising 'white' wine is made solely from pinot noir grapes. It's fresh, zingy and clean in taste, but also surprisingly full bodied. Very good value.

Specialist wine stores or www.richmondplains.co.nz

Chardonnay

'Shar-don-ay'

It's hard to find a chardonnay that stands out from the crowd at the best of times, but in this price range it is nigh on impossible, unless you look and taste extremely widely. Great-value, low-priced chardonnays do exist, but they are few and far between.

Chardonnay has been knocked off its perch as the second most-planted grape in New Zealand (actually it was neck-and-neck with pinot noir). Once number-one most planted grape in this country, chardonnay is now third place-getter in the New Zealand national vineyard statistics, trailing sauvignon blanc and pinot noir.

If you love chardonnay but tire of it after one or two glasses, try choosing from the increasing range of highly rated 'unoaked' versions in this year's guide. The reason these wines have generally fared far better than many (though not all, it must be noted) of the other chardonnays here is that they are far more true to what good chardonnay should taste like. And, unfettered by oak or over-the-top creamy and buttery flavours, these unoaked chardonnays will harness a whole new following for the grape and wine that is still the undisputed queen of the wine world and one of the world's most widely grown and best-known grape varieties.

Chardonnay grapes originated in Burgundy, France, where they are responsible for a wide range of wine styles, from crisp, slightly austere chablis to big-bodied, more distinctive expressions of the grape. Chardonnay grapes are used not only to make dry white wine but also to create some of the world's best dessert wines. It is also one of the three classic grape varieties used to make champagne and many of the best sparkling wines in the world.

Star chardonnay

2006 Lonestone Hawke's Bay Chardonnay

$20 ☆☆☆☆

2006 Akarua Unoaked Chardonnay **$23–24** ☆☆☆☆ Screwcap

As unoaked chardonnays go, this is a big, weighty and satisfying wine. Extremely well made, with lovely balance and a long finish. Great value.

🛒 Specialist wine stores or www.akarua.com

2007 Allan Scott Marlborough Chardonnay
$22–23 ☆☆☆½ Screwcap

South Island chardonnay that is as accessibly soft, smooth and easy to enjoy as it is widely available. This wine is citrusy and fresh, with hints of creaminess but never over the top in style. Good value.

🛒 Widely available

2006 Allan Scott Wallops Marlborough Chardonnay
$18–20 ☆☆☆☆ Screwcap

High-quality, well-crafted Marlborough chardonnay from one of the region's best-known and most established winemakers. Very good wine.

🛒 Specialist wine stores

2007 Anchorage Unoaked Chardonnay **$18–20** ☆☆☆½ Screwcap

This wine might sport the label 'unoaked', but it's a pretty full-bodied white wine with overt citrusy flavours and hints of rounded aroma and taste. It is a nicely balanced dry white wine. Serve lightly chilled.

🛒 Specialist wine stores or www.anchoragewines.co.nz

2005 Askerne Hawke's Bay Chardonnay $20–21 ☆☆☆½

Easy-to-love Hawke's Bay dry white with all the bells and whistles on every chardonnay lover's wish list. Creamy, full bodied with a citrusy tang, it is good with roasted hapuka or roast chicken.

Specialist wine stores or www.askerne.co.nz

2005 Bach 22 Chardonnay $13–14 ☆☆☆½ Screwcap

If you're at the beach this summer, take a bottle of this to enjoy in the shade. It is a great-value dry white wine with rounded, medium body and hints of tropical fruit flavour.

Widely available

2006 Bensen Block Gisborne Unoaked Chardonnay $16–17 ☆☆☆☆ Screwcap

Exceptionally fresh, lovely Gisborne chardonnay that breaks the mould of over-the-top chardonnays with its clean, citrusy aromas and taste. Love it – especially at this price.

Widely available

2006 Blackenbrook Nelson Chardonnay $22–23 ☆☆☆½ Screwcap

Like most New Zealand wineries, this little Nelson one is so small that you do have to search hard to find their wines, but yes, they are worth looking for. The 2006 and 2007 whites from Blackenbrook are smothered in medals due to their lively, intense concentration of flavour. Very good value for money.

Specialist wine stores in Nelson and Auckland, or www.blackenbrook.co.nz

2006 Bouldevines Dogpoint Road Chardonnay $18–19 ☆☆☆ Screwcap

Light, fruity chardonnay made with grapes grown in New

Zealand's largest wine region, Marlborough. Hints of spice from overt oak influence add body and flavour interest.

🛒 Widely available

2007 Cape Campbell Marlborough Chardonnay

$18–19 ☆☆☆☆ Screwcap

Here's a great example of a lower-priced chardonnay being a purer example of a classic wine. This lovely Marlborough chardonnay may not have all the big, bold, buttery nuances, but it's all the better for its fresh zing and lingering citrusy taste. Love it.

🛒 Liquor stores or www.capecampbell.co.nz

2007 Cape Campbell Marlborough Limited Edition Reserve Chardonnay **$24–25** ☆☆☆½ Screwcap

It's as clean as a whistle in style and full of big, buttery flavours typical of many South Island chardonnays. Good value for a big-bodied, easy-to-drink style – for posh everyday drinking or with a great Sunday roast chook.

🛒 Liquor stores or www.capecampbell.co.nz

2007 Church Road Chardonnay **$22–23** ☆☆☆½ Screwcap

It's bright, citrusy and all too drinkable. A well-made Hawke's Bay chardonnay with all the bells and whistles of fresh fruit and spicy oak flavours and a full body.

🛒 Widely available

2007 Clearview Unwooded Chardonnay Hawke's Bay

$18–20 ☆☆☆½ Screwcap

This chardonnay may be unwooded but it's not short on body, freshness or flavour; it owns these three qualities and more in abundance. It also has great length of flavour and is great value.

🛒 Specialist wine stores or www.clearviewestate.co.nz

2006 Cockatoo Ridge Chardonnay **$12–13** ☆☆☆ Screwcap

A big-name, simple Australian chardonnay that is light, fresh and clean. Good for taking to the beach.

Widely available

2005 Commissioner's Block Chardonnay **$16–17** ☆☆☆ Screwcap

Easy-drinking, full-flavoured, everyday chardonnay with lots of spicy oak flavours.

Specialist wine stores

2006 Corbans Private Bin Hawke's Bay Chardonnay
$20–22 ☆☆☆½ Screwcap

This is a big but elegant chardonnay from Hawke's Bay; home to more top Kiwi chardonnays than any other region. It's full of subtle flavours of rock melon, soft tropical fruit and nectarine tastes. A lovely special-occasion New Zealand chardonnay.

Widely available

2007 Crawford Farm Unoaked Chardonnay
$20–22 ☆☆☆☆ Screwcap

Great stuff, this unoaked chardonnay. It offers all the appeal of a classy dry white wine, with soft mouthfeel and appealingly varietal citrus flavours – chardonnay all the way, without oak, and that allows this wine to shine. Great value.

Widely available

2006 Crossroads Hawke's Bay Destination Series Chardonnay
$19–20 ☆☆☆ Screwcap

Tropical-tasting, light everyday chardonnay with an oaky finish to add length and body.

Widely available

2006 Dashwood Chardonnay $19–20 ☆☆☆½ Screwcap

This great-value everyday chardonnay from Marlborough over-delivers on flavour. Soft, rounded and fresh.

Widely available or www.vavasour.com

2006 Drylands Marlborough Chardonnay
$19–20 ☆☆☆½ Screwcap

Buttery but fresh Marlborough chardonnay with overt citrus flavours. Great everyday drinking for chardonnay lovers. It's a good price for a well-made wine.

Widely available

2006 Esk Valley Hawke's Bay Chardonnay
$20–21 ☆☆☆½ Screwcap

This is a full-bodied, rounded Hawke's Bay chardonnay, with nectarine, peach and melon flavours in a fruit-forward style.

Widely available

2006 Five Flax Chardonnay $10–12 ☆☆☆½ Screwcap

Here's a light, soft, everyday chardonnay. It has creamy smoothness and easy citrusy flavours that marry well with roast pork or chicken.

Widely available

2005 Forrest Estate Marlborough Chardonnay
$19–20 ☆☆☆½ Screwcap

Talk about a tutti-frutti chardonnay – this is clean, tropical in taste and long on the finish. Everything that you want for a special treat – and more, due to its clean and long finish.

Widely available or www.forrestwines.co.nz

2007 Freefall Marlborough Chardonnay $20–21 ☆☆☆½ Screwcap

This South Island chardonnay offers lots of body (it's medium to full bodied in style) as well as spicy flavours and a creamy finish. This wine is good for chardonnay lovers for everyday drinking or as a pre-dinner party wine.

Specialist wine stores

2007 Goldridge Estate Gisborne Chardonnay $18–19 ☆☆☆ Screwcap

The Goldridge Estate winery is based in Matakana, an hour's drive north of Auckland, but this wine is made with big, bold chardonnay grapes grown in Gisborne. Rounded, full and creamy, this is a drink-now white.

Specialist wine stores

2005 Goldridge Estate Hawke's Bay Barrique Matured Chardonnay $18–19 ☆☆☆ Screwcap

Goldridge Estate winery might be at Matakana, but that doesn't mean all its wines are made with locally grown grapes. This Hawke's Bay chardonnay has a rounded, full-bodied style with creamy flavours – good for those who like their chardonnays big and bold.

Specialist wine stores

2006 Hardys Nottage Hill Chardonnay $9–10 ☆☆☆ Screwcap

Big-name, medium-bodied chardonnay with light fruity flavours. Always good value for a simple, clean dry white wine.

Widely available

2007 Hay Maker Hawke's Bay Chardonnay $18–20 ☆☆☆½ Screwcap

Hawke's Bay is the most consistent region in New Zealand for good chardonnay at all price levels, which translates through to a rounded, full-bodied everyday wine with creamy nuances and fresh flavours.

🛒 Specialist wine stores

2007 Hunter's Marlborough Chardonnay $19–20 ☆☆☆☆ Screwcap

Here's a bright, fresh and extremely well-balanced chardonnay. It's the open citrusy flavours I like most here – and the long finish. A really good wine with food – try it with barbecued fresh game fish – or drink it before dinner with good nuts and light cheese.

🛒 Widely available

2006 Jackson Estate Shelter Belt Chardonnay
$22–23 ☆☆☆½ Screwcap

One of the most restrained, fresh, zingy Marlborough chardonnays about at this price. It has all the bells and whistles – creamy taste, full body, noticeable oak taste – of good chardonnay, but it's far better balanced than most. Like it.

🛒 Widely available

2006 Jacob's Creek Chardonnay $13–14 ☆☆☆ Screwcap

It's a big-name, well-known, everyday sort of label, but this wine delivers lively, lovely fresh-tasting chardonnay. It's good value too.

🛒 Widely available

2004 Kaikoura Marlborough Chardonnay $19–20 ☆☆☆ Screwcap

If you're on the lookout for a big, buttery southern chardonnay, here it is. Kaikoura is the label and Marlborough the region in which the grapes in this wine were grown. Average value.

🛒 Specialist wine stores or www.kaikourawinery.co.nz

2005 Kew Barrel Fermented Chardonnay

$22–23 ☆☆☆½ Screwcap

Like most New Zealand barrel-fermented chardonnays, this wine is full bodied, full of flavour and needs big food flavours to accompany it. Chill lightly and enjoy with Nelson oysters or your favourite shellfish.

Specialist wine stores or email info@kew.co.nz

2005 Kew Chardonnay **$15–16** ☆☆☆½ Screwcap

This is the most straightforward of all four Kew chardonnays in this chapter. Fresh, citrusy Gisborne fruit flavours with a touch of spicy oak make for a good everyday wine.

Specialist wine stores or email info@kew.co.nz

2004 Kew Unwooded Chardonnay **$22–23** ☆☆☆½ Screwcap

Talk about the chardonnay capital of New Zealand. That's the title Gisborne winemakers have adopted for themselves, and Anita Ewart-Coy from Kew Wines is no exception – with four chardonnays in this chapter. This wine is the oldest of the four – a full-bodied, creamy big white ready to drink now with its rich fruit flavours. Team it up with roast pork and all the trimmings.

Specialist wine stores or email info@kew.co.nz

2006 Kew Virgin Chardonnay **$22–23** ☆☆☆ Screwcap

Fresh young Gisborne chardonnay with vibrant, citrusy flavours of lemon and grapefruit and a rounded, medium-bodied style.

Specialist wine stores or email info@kew.co.nz

2007 Kim Crawford Unoaked Chardonnay

$19–20 ☆☆☆½ Screwcap

Described as a forward-drinking style by winemaker Kim Crawford, this chardonnay is crisp and clean as well as being packed with fruit flavours. It's a good lunchtime or late-afternoon wine – drink before dinner.

🛒 Widely available and at Glengarry stores in the North Island

2005 Kono Marlborough Unoaked Chardonnay
$16–17 ☆☆☆½ Screwcap

This is a fresh, light chardonnay because of its 'unoaked' style and screwcap. An easy, medium-bodied everyday white with citrus flavours.

🛒 Liquor stores or www.kono-nz.com

2007 Lake Chalice Marlborough Chardonnay
$19–20 ☆☆☆½ Screwcap

Like many Marlborough chardonnays, this one is positively oozing body and buttery flavours coupled with zingy acids. A good wine to drink with food.

🛒 Specialist wine stores or www.lakechalice.com

2007 Lake Chalice Marlborough Flight 42 Unoaked Chardonnay $20–21 ☆☆☆☆ Screwcap

If you're a wine purist, then it's chardonnays like this that often appeal more than the overt, big buttery numbers. I love the fresh, clean, citrusy fruit flavours of this wine, coupled with the zingy, lingering finish. Very good.

🛒 Specialist wine stores or www.lakechalice.com

2006 Laroche Chardonnay $16–17 ☆☆☆ Screwcap

This southern French chardonnay is intended for everyday drinking, hence its fruity upfront flavours, soft acids and easy drinking style.

🛒 Glengarry stores in the North Island and specialist wine stores nationwide

2004 Lawson's Dry Hills Marlborough Chardonnay

$22–23 ☆☆☆½ Screwcap

Four years old but still fresh, this Marlborough chardonnay tastes a real treat with slow-roasted lemon chicken. Its own citrusy lemon aromas and flavours marry well with the food, as well as being more than satisfying on their own.

Widely available

2007 Lawson's Dry Hills Marlborough Unoaked Chardonnay

$22–23 ☆☆☆½ Screwcap

The unoaked chardonnay trend continues unabated, if the success of this wine is anything to go by. Popular for its relative lightness, this wine is all about fresh lemon and grapefruit flavours with a vibrant style.

Widely available

Star chardonnay

2006 Lonestone Hawke's Bay Chardonnay

$20 ☆☆☆☆ Screwcap

At last, a chardonnay that's low in price but big in value. Made from grapes grown in Hawke's Bay, this is a brilliantly balanced, full-bodied chardonnay that subtly offers all the usual bells and whistles in a more restrained style than the vast majority. It's fantastic value.

Specialist wine stores or contact Bennett & Deller for stockists near you, phone (09) 378 9463

2007 Longridge Hawke's Bay Chardonnay $14–15 ☆☆☆

It's one of the oldest chardonnay brands around in New Zealand today – a soft, smooth wine but simple and fruity. Everyday drinking and reliably fresh at this price.

Widely available

2006 Maimai Creek Chardonnay $15–16 ☆☆☆ Screwcap

This is a very good Hawke's Bay chardonnay, with a rounded, full body and stonefruit flavours.

Online at www.maimaicreek.com

2006 Main Divide Chardonnay $19–20 ☆☆☆½ Screwcap

A big, instantly recognisable chardonnay from grapes grown in the South Island and made at the Pegasus Bay winery in Waipara, North Canterbury.

Specialist wine stores or www.maindivide.com

2007 Main Divide Chardonnay $20–21 ☆☆☆☆ Screwcap

Here's a classy dry white, from its big burgundy bottle to its rounded full body and fresh citrus flavours. It has a long finish, offering great value for this price.

Liquor stores and specialist wine stores or www.pegasusbay.com

2007 Matahiwi Estate Hawke's Bay Unoaked Chardonnay $18–19 ☆☆☆½ Screwcap

Good-value Hawke's Bay chardonnay in a fresh, bright style with rounded peachy fruit characters – over-delivers on value for money.

Specialist wine stores or www.matahiwi.co.nz

2007 Maven Marlborough Chardonnay $18–20 ☆☆☆½ Screwcap

Another beautifully evocative label from this innovative Marlborough wine company – and a good chardonnay to boot. This is a big but just slightly buttery South Island chardonnay.

🛒 Specialist wine stores or www.mavenwines.co.nz

2007 Mission Estate Hawke's Bay Chardonnay

$16–18 ☆☆☆½ Screwcap

Fresh as a daisy or just as fresh as a young, citrusy, nicely balanced chardonnay. Oh, and great value too.

🛒 Widely available

2007 Mission Vineyard Selection Clifton Road Chardonnay

$19–20 ☆☆☆ Screwcap

Here's a big, buttery chardonnay that contrasts wildly with the citrusy fresh Mission Estate chardonnay above (which is itself a more balanced wine). This is for fans of OTT chardonnays.

🛒 Widely available

2007 Moana Park Hawke's Bay Chardonnay

$17–18 ☆☆☆½ Screwcap

Hawke's Bay is home to some of the best chardonnays in New Zealand at all prices, including this lovely, everyday, fresh, citrus-tasting dry white. Chill lightly and enjoy.

🛒 Specialist wine stores or email sales@moanapark.co.nz

2005 Moana Park Vineyard Tribute Chardonnay

$24–25 ☆☆☆½ Screwcap

Talk about a big, buttery Hawke's Bay chardonnay. This wine has all the rounded peachy, stonefruit flavours you look for in a chardonnay, coupled with an overtly full-bodied style.

🛒 Specialist wine stores

2007 Momo Chardonnay $19–20 ☆☆☆½ Screwcap

A citrusy, clean, lively chardonnay with a lovely fresh everyday style – better than most at this price by a country mile (or three). Buy it.

Widely available

Monkey Bay Unoaked Gisborne Chardonnay

$10–12 ☆☆☆ Screwcap

This fresh non-vintage chardonnay from Gisborne tastes dry, clean and fruity. A good-value beginner's white wine.

Widely available

2007 Montana Gisborne Chardonnay $16–17 ☆☆☆½ Screwcap

It might be mass made but this wine is admirable in its restraint – or rather the winemaker's restraint. It's citrusy and fresh and allowed to shine as chardonnay, which is great news at this price. Buy lots as an everyday drinking dry white.

Widely available

2006 Montana Reserve Marlborough Chardonnay

$20–22 ☆☆☆½ Screwcap

It's big, creamy and packed with rich tropical fruit flavours of pineapple, grapefruit and lemon.

Widely available

2006 Morton Estate Hawke's Bay Chardonnay

$19–20 ☆☆☆☆ Screwcap

This Hawke's Bay chardonnay falls under the 'everyday white label' from Morton Estate. It may be made for simple pleasures, but this wine over-delivers on value for money. Buy lots to enjoy with or without food.

Widely available

2006 Mud House Marlborough Chardonnay

$18–20 ☆☆☆½ Screwcap

Here's a lively, clean, great-value everyday chardonnay that shows lots of fruit-driven flavours, retaining winemaking restraint too – which makes this wine as nice a drink on its own as with food.

🛒 Specialist wine stores

2006 Mud House Swan Marlborough Chardonnay

$19–20 ☆☆☆½ Screwcap

If you're a fan of big, citrusy, full-flavoured chardonnays, this Marlborough version will deliver everything you want – and more – for everyday drinking. It's good value for money and such a bold style that it works better with food than without.

🛒 Specialist wine stores

2006 Mystery Creek Gisborne Chardonnay

$16–17 ☆☆☆½ Screwcap

A rounded, buttery style of Gisborne chardonnay with all the appealing bells and whistles that Kiwi chardonnay fans have come to expect. This is a wine to drink now with a very soft finish. It also tastes best either on its own or with snacks rather than a meal – its acids are relatively soft, lending it an easy-drinking style.

🛒 Specialist wine stores or www.mysterycreekwines.com

2004 Mystery Creek Reserve Chardonnay $24–25 ☆☆☆☆ Screwcap

Big creamy and caramel aromas lead into a full-bodied, noticeably oak-influenced chardonnay. I like the body and the fresh acids on the finish, which add a cleansing aspect to this otherwise very voluptuous, full-on chardonnay. A well-balanced wine for very satisfactory everyday drinking – could well be great value for money, especially if under $20.

🛒 Specialist wine stores or www.mysterycreekwines.com

2005 Mystery Creek Reserve Chardonnay $24–25 ☆☆☆☆ Screwcap

This is a relatively youthful-tasting Kiwi chardonnay and very different in style from the more developed, easier to drink now, 2004 version above. By contrast, this wine has higher, more vibrant acid structure and a fresh, clean palate, making it an easy wine to partner with foods – particularly Sunday's roast chicken. Both the 2004 and 2005 versions offer good value for money.

Specialist wine stores or www.mysterycreekwines.com

2007 One Tree Hawke's Bay Chardonnay $20-21 ☆☆☆½

Fresh, bright, creamy chardonnay with lively citrus flavours and a medium body. Made for everyday enjoyment.

Specialist wine stores or www.craggyrange.com

2004 Orlando St Hilary Padthaway Chardonnay
$17–18 ☆☆☆ Screwcap

Big, buttery Australian chardonnay with all the bells and whistles. It's getting on a little now, at four years old, and definitely a with-food wine. Drink with creamy Nelson oysters, roast chicken or baked salmon.

Widely available

2006 Renato Nelson Chardonnay $24–25 ☆☆☆ Screwcap

Lovers of big, buttery chardonnays will enjoy this Nelson number, made in small quantities. It's unmistakably chardonnay from the first whiff to the last sip, but would be great with a little less overt creamy taste.

Specialist wine stores or www.renatoestate.co.nz

2006 Richmond Plains Nelson Chardonnay
$19–20 ☆☆☆½ Screwcap

Richmond Plains winery is one of many tiny Kiwi wineries, but the quality of its wines is high. Fresh, citrusy and nicely balanced with soft flavours, this is a deliciously good chardonnay – in quality, value and lingering finish.

Specialist wine stores or www.richmondplains.co.nz

2007 Rongopai Seasonal Chardonnay $14–15 ☆☆☆½ Screwcap

Fresh, bright and light, this North Island chardonnay tastes of citrusy flavours in the lemon and grapefruit spectrum, with a medium-length finish. Good value at this price.

New World and Pak'nSave supermarkets

2006 Rose Tree Cottage Gisborne Chardonnay
$23–24 ☆☆☆½ Screwcap

This is an instantly recognisable Gisborne chardonnay with its big butterscotch aromas, rounded body and zingy finish. Chill lightly and enjoy with roast pork and apple sauce, which will pick up on the off-dry flavours here.

Widely available

2007 Saint Clair Marlborough Chardonnay
$16–17 ☆☆☆½ Screwcap

At this price, this chardonnay over-delivers on value for money, flavour and length at the end of each mouthful. Creamy, citrusy flavours combine with a clean, fresh, lingering ending.

Widely available

2007 Saints Gisborne Chardonnay $17–18 ☆☆☆½ Screwcap

Big, rounded, creamy chardonnay for lovers of this grape. Drink it lightly chilled to tone down the cedary aromas, and enjoy with fish tangine.

Widely available

2006 Sanctuary Marlborough Chardonnay $13–14 ☆☆☆ Screwcap

This is a simple, off-dry, everyday chardonnay that will easily sate the appetites of wine drinkers looking for a quick after-work glass.

🛒 Widely available

2005 Sandalford Margaret River Chardonnay
$24–25 ☆☆☆½ Screwcap

Fans of big, rounded chardonnays will love this Western Australian version with its spicy, overt buttery and tropical fruit flavours. It has a soft, long finish.

🛒 Specialist wine stores or www.sandalford.com

2006 Sandalford Protégé Chardonnay $19–20 ☆☆☆ Screwcap

Another full-bodied, big-tasting Western Australian chardonnay – great with buttery roast chook in mid-winter.

🛒 Specialist wine stores or www.sandalford.com

2006 Selaks Favourite Hawke's Bay Chardonnay
$20–21 ☆☆☆½ Screwcap

A soft, rounded Hawke's Bay chardonnay for everyday drinking.

🛒 Widely available

2006 Selaks Marlborough Chardonnay $14–15 ☆☆☆ Screwcap

This big-name, widely available Marlborough chardonnay is a simple everyday white wine – just off-dry to add appeal.

🛒 Widely available

2005 Shipwreck Bay Chardonnay $15–17 ☆☆☆ Screwcap

Big, soft, full-bodied Kiwi chardonnay. Simple but satisfying for chardonnay lovers.

🛒 Widely available

2007 Sileni Cellar Selection Hawke's Bay Chardonnay

$19–20 ☆☆☆ Screwcap

A light, everyday Hawke's Bay chardonnay with a slightly short finish but an attractive-enough style for a daytime or late-afternoon glass.

Liquor stores and specialist wine stores

2006 Southbank Estate Hawke's Bay Chardonnay

$19–20 ☆☆☆

It might be a year older than its more youthful sibling below, but the style of chardonnay is the same – big, buttery and creamy. It is more about appealing to wine drinkers who love this style than the more restrained citrusy wines of Hawke's Bay. It tastes best with food and will easily find fans.

Specialist wine stores or www.southbankestate.com

2007 Southbank Estate Hawke's Bay Chardonnay $19–20 ☆☆☆

Big, buttery, creamy Hawke's Bay chardonnay – good for everyday drinking but better with food than without, which will help to tame its overtly buttery overtones.

Specialist wine stores or www.southbankestate.com

2006 Spinyback Nelson Chardonnay $14–15 ☆☆☆½ Screwcap

This chardonnay from the Nelson-based Waimea Estates winery is light, crisp and lemon in taste, and at this price is very good value for money for an everyday drinking white. Especially good with pan-fried fresh fish.

Liquor stores or www.waimeaestates.co.nz

2006 Spy Valley Marlborough Chardonnay

$19–20 ☆☆☆½ Screwcap

The 2006 vintage delivered some of the tastiest South Island chardonnays in the last half-decade. This is a fresh citrusy wine with lively acids – matches really well with roast chicken.

Widely available

2007 Stoneleigh Marlborough Chardonnay

$18–20 ☆☆☆☆ Screwcap

Like so many good South Island wines, this big-name chardonnay is driven by rich, bold fruit flavours. It's a stunning wine for everyday drinking, over-delivering on flavour, value and – now that it has a screwcap – reliability. Buy it.

Widely available

2007 Stoneleigh Rapaura Series Chardonnay

$23–24 ☆☆☆½ Screwcap

Marlborough might be home to more sauvignon blanc than chardonnay, but wines like this still have a massive following. It's big, buttery, rounded and full bodied. At this price it offers good value but should definitely be consumed with food.

Widely available

2006 Stone Paddock Hawke's Bay Chardonnay

$18–20 ☆☆☆½ Screwcap

This is a medium-bodied and medium-flavoured Hawke's Bay chardonnay; lively in style with clean, fresh flavours of tropical and stonefruit and a light finish.

Specialist wine stores or www.paritua.com

2006 Tapestry McLaren Vale Chardonnay $19–20 ☆☆☆ Screwcap

Australian chardonnay which is rounded, full and buttery as anything. A good everyday drink; serve chilled.

Widely available

2006 Taylors Clare Valley Chardonnay $18–20 ☆☆☆ Screwcap

This is a fresh, citrusy, slightly creamy-tasting chardonnay – made for everyday drinking and delivering on that promise with ease.

Widely available

2007 Taylors Eighty Acres Chardonnay Viognier

$19–20 ☆☆☆½ Screwcap

It might be an unusual blend, using chardonnay and viognier in the same wine, but it works here, adding lifted perfumed peachy aromas and an appealing off-dry taste for everyday drinking and newcomers to wine. Serve lightly chilled.

Widely available

2006 Taylors Promised Land Unwooded Chardonnay

$16–18 ☆☆☆½ Screwcap

Wines like this big-namer from Australia show why chardonnay is the world's most popular white wine. Fresh, citrusy and rounded, it delivers everything you want in a chardonnay. Great value too.

Widely available

2007 Te Awa Left Field Hawke's Bay Chardonnay

$22–23 ☆☆☆½ Screwcap

Everything you want in a chardonnay is all right here – full body, citrusy, clean lemon flavours and a long finish – it's a tasty, great-value wine from the heart of New Zealand's best chardonnay region, Hawke's Bay.

Widely available

2007 Te Awa Windmill Chardonnay

$19–20 ☆☆☆½ Screwcap

As everyday chardonnays go, this Hawke's Bay version gains lots of its appeal from being just off-dry – that light body and slight hint of sweet tropical fruit flavours provide nicely rounded curves in the mouth.

Liquor stores or www.teawa.com

2006 Te Mania Nelson Chardonnay $19–20 ☆☆☆½ Screwcap

From a really small Nelson winery comes this lively, fresh chardonnay with its full-bodied style and citrusy flavours. It's good value too.

Specialist wine stores

2006 Te Mania Nelson Reserve Chardonnay
$19–20 ☆☆☆½ Screwcap

Here's the big, buttery sibling to the chardonnay above. It's bigger in body, style and taste, offering diversity for those looking for a more robust white wine. Drink with roast chicken on a Sunday night.

Specialist wine stores

2007 Thornbury Gisborne Chardonnay $20–21 ☆☆☆½ Screwcap

This is a chardonnay for all those who love big, buttery numbers, of which Gisborne has plenty. It's full bodied, rich in flavour and long on the finish – drink a little on its own with good nibbles or, better still, pair it up with a rosemary-infused roast chicken.

Widely available

2006 Thorn Clarke Sandpiper Eden Valley Chardonnay
$19–20 ☆☆☆½ Screwcap

South Australian chardonnay at its best here – especially at this price. This is a fresh, clean, citrusy chardonnay with rounded mouthfeel and zingy acids holding it all in check. Lovely balance and great value for money.

Widely available

2005 Three Stones Hawke's Bay Chardonnay

$19–20 ☆☆☆☆ Screwcap

The body is rounded, the flavours are of stonefruit and the finish is long. This provides excellent value for money and is deliciously good for everyday drinking. Soft, smooth, clean and ripe.

🛒 Widely available

2006 Timara Oak Aged Chardonnay $12–13 ☆☆☆ Screwcap

This is an entry-level chardonnay with off-dry flavours of grapefruit, peach and nectarine. Chill it and enjoy at the beach or a party.

🛒 Widely available

2007 Tohu Gisborne Unoaked Chardonnay

$19–20 ☆☆☆½ Screwcap

It's easy to see why unoaked chardonnays have taken off; wines like this one offer all the vibrant, citrusy flavours you expect in chardonnay, in an elegant wine.

🛒 Specialist wine stores or www.tohuwines.co.nz

2006 Tohu Marlborough Unoaked Chardonnay

$19–20 ☆☆☆½ Screwcap

This is a light style of chardonnay with bright citrusy fruit flavours and a fresh, lively and lingering finish.

🛒 Specialist wine stores or www.tohuwines.co.nz

2006 Trapiche Oak Cask Chardonnay $15–16 ☆☆☆

Big Argentinian chardonnay with lots of spicy, savoury oak flavours and full body.

🛒 Selected supermarkets, liquor stores and specialist wine stores

2006 Trapiche Roble Chardonnay $15–16 ☆☆☆½

A nicely rounded Argentinian chardonnay with citrusy and spicy flavours. Really fresh, clean and good value for money too.

🛒 Selected supermarkets, liquor stores and specialist wine stores

2007 Trinity Hill Hawke's Bay Chardonnay

$22–23 ☆☆☆☆ Screwcap

Great value-for-money chardonnays hardly come better than this mid-North Island version. With its creamy, rounded body and citrusy flavours all kept in balance by ripe fruit flavours, this is exceptionally good everyday drinking – and chardonnay purists will enjoy it with posh cheese or a good roast chook.

🛒 Widely available or www.trinityhill.com

2007 Tuki Tuki Road Chardonnay $20–22 ☆☆☆☆ Screwcap

Fans of full-bodied chardonnays will love this big, rounded, creamy-tasting Hawke's Bay white. It's nicely balanced with crisp, fresh citrus flavours and a long finish. Very good value.

🛒 Specialist wine stores

2007 Twin Islands Chardonnay $19–20 ☆☆☆☆ Screwcap

Talk about a great chardonnay at the price. This is a lovely, lively and personality-filled dry white wine, with great balance of flavour. Good value is harder to come by in an everyday chardonnay.

🛒 Widely available

2006 Vavasour Awatere Valley Chardonnay

$24–25 ☆☆☆½ Screwcap

Vavasour winery is the oldest in the fast-growing Awatere Valley in Marlborough – where this wine comes from. Its cool nights and hot days give distinctive flavours to grapes, which create wines like this linear, crisp chardonnay. This one over-delivers on flavour and value.

Specialist wine stores and liquor stores or www.vavasour.com

2007 Vidal Hawke's Bay Chardonnay $18–19 ☆☆☆½ Screwcap

Hawke's Bay's best white wine that is widely available is definitely chardonnay, and this peachy, fresh, nicely balanced big white is a good example of that. Good value too.

Widely available

2007 Villa Maria Cellar Selection Hawke's Bay Chardonnay
$22–23 ☆☆☆½ Screwcap

Yes, you're dead right – there are two chardonnays in Villa Maria's 'cellar selection' series: one from Marlborough (below) and this more rounded, stonefruit-flavoured wine from Hawke's Bay. This is my pick by a long shot for its soft, smooth flavours and rounded mouthfeel. Both wines are very good value, in their own distinct styles.

Widely available

2007 Villa Maria Cellar Selection Marlborough Chardonnay
$22–23 ☆☆☆½ Screwcap

This South Island chardonnay is the Marlborough equivalent of the wine above, and is a lively, citrusy and big-bodied wine with lots of fresh flavours such as lemon, grapefruit and a creamy finish.

Widely available

2007 Villa Maria East Coast Chardonnay $17–18 ☆☆☆ Screwcap

Here's a light, fresh chardonnay made with grapes grown in the North Island. It's fresh, bright and light – made for everyday drinking.

Widely available

2007 Waimea Bolitho Nelson Chardonnay
$24–25 ☆☆☆ Screwcap

This is a big, rounded, creamy Nelson chardonnay with lovely refined citrusy flavours and a long finish. Good value, if you're pushing the boat out and want a special white wine. Drink with roast pork.

Liquor stores or www.waimeaestates.co.nz

2006 Waimea Nelson Chardonnay $18–20 ☆☆☆½ Screwcap

Rounded, full-bodied Nelson chardonnay with bright, fresh, citrusy characters and a lingering finish. Good value.

Specialist wine stores or www.waimeaestates.co.nz

2007 Waipara Hills Marlborough Chardonnay
$19–20 ☆☆☆ Screwcap

You need to read the fine print to see for sure that this wine is separate and distinct from its sibling (below); the only difference is the most major one – the origin of the grapes that are in this wine. This is rounder, fuller bodied and less citrusy and bright. Still good value but a different style from its sister chardonnay below.

Specialist wine stores and Glengarry stores in the North Island

2007 Waipara Hills Waipara Chardonnay $19–20 ☆☆☆½ Screwcap

Lovely, lively North Canterbury chardonnay with a beautiful balance of crisp, refreshing citrusy flavours, acid and zing – all of which balance the hint of creaminess in this chardonnay.

Specialist wine stores and Glengarry stores in the North Island

2006 Wairau River Marlborough Chardonnay
$19–20 ☆☆☆☆ Screwcap

At the risk of sounding like a wine geek, it's the structure of this bright, fresh Marlborough chardonnay that gives it an edge.

Fruit-driven in taste and full bodied, it has lovely firm acids that stretch out the fruit flavours to a long, long finish. Very good value.

🛒 Widely available or www.wairauriverwines.co.nz

2007 Wild Rock Chardonnay $20 ☆☆☆☆ Screwcap

It's refreshing to find a big-bodied chardonnay with such subtlety of flavour; smooth and creamy, hints of citrusy freshness lurk in every sip of this wine, which is beautifully rounded and easy to drink. Great value too.

🛒 Specialist wine stores or www.craggyrange.com

2006 Wyndham Estate Bin 222 Chardonnay $16–18 ☆☆☆ Screwcap

Big-name wine but simple style; off-dry with hints of sweet pineapple and citrus flavours. Now it has a screwcap, this big, bold Aussie chardonnay is a good reliable stand-by for everyday white wine drinking.

🛒 Widely available

2006 Zilzie Chardonnay $18–19 ☆☆☆

Big, ripe, citrusy and buttery chardonnay with loads of flavour and an affordable price tag. Good everyday drinking.

🛒 Specialist wine stores

2007 Zilzie Selection 23 Chardonnay $15–16 ☆☆☆ Screwcap

Big, buttery Australian chardonnays are among the most popular white wines in the world – and here is an extremely affordable version. Lightly chill it to tone down its overt personality, then serve with roast chook.

🛒 Liquor stores, selected supermarkets and specialist wine stores

Frascati

'Fras-cart-ee'

2006 Solepapa Frascati Superiore Piccini $14–15 ☆☆☆

A popular and successful white wine in New Zealand, especially in restaurants. This is light, soft and slightly spicy.

Mostly restaurants or for stockists contact Prodotti d'Italia, phone (09) 276 7140 or www.pdi.co.nz

Gewürztraminer

'Give-urtz-tram-een-er'

Gewürztraminer might be hard to pronounce but it is one of the most instantly recognisable wines. It is incredibly easy to love, and there are now a growing number of great gewürztraminers being made in New Zealand.

The grape all but died out in this country but is now growing again, not only in quantity but also in quality. The country's best, Vinoptima, is way above the price threshold for inclusion in this guide (unless you were drinking just one glass), but shows that New Zealand has the potential to produce top-notch gewürztraminers, as do the highly drinkable wines in this chapter.

This very easy to recognise wine style is made from incredibly sensitive grapes that are vulnerable to wind and cool weather. Despite the fact that gewürztraminer is difficult to grow – and almost impossible for many people to pronounce – this is one of New Zealand's up-and-coming white wine stars.

Star gewürztraminer

2007 Montana Riverpoint Gisborne Matawhero Gewürztraminer

$24–25 ☆☆☆½

2007 Anchorage Classic Gewürztraminer Nelson

$16–18 ☆☆☆½ Screwcap

This is one very promising Nelson winery. Small it may be, but its riesling, pinot gris and this luscious gewürztraminer are all superb examples of aromatic white wines. I love the balance, zing and lingering flavour in each mouthful.

Specialist wine stores or www.anchoragewines.co.nz

2006 Askerne Gewürztraminer $22–23 ☆☆☆½ Screwcap

This Hawke's Bay gewürztraminer is luscious, rich and packed with floral aromas and flavours.

Specialist wine stores or www.askerne.co.nz

2007 Cape Campbell Marlborough Limited Edition Reserve Gewürztraminer $24–25 ☆☆☆½ Screwcap

Talk about a dead ringer for luscious, rose-flavoured Turkish delight. Love the pure floral flavours, the hint of sweet aromatic grapiness and the long, long finish. Great value.

Liquor stores or www.capecampbell.co.nz

2006 Clearview Estate Gewürztraminer $22–24 ☆☆☆½ Screwcap

To describe this Gisborne gewürztraminer as luscious is to wildly understate its intense aromatics and lively spice and old-fashioned rose aromas – all right, enough of the rave. Serve it lightly chilled with salted pistachios in the sunshine.

Specialist wine stores or www.clearviewestate.co.nz

2006 Corbans Private Bin Hawke's Bay Gewürztraminer $22–24 ☆☆☆ Screwcap

This wine reflects what good gewürztraminer is all about: it's big in aroma (Turkish delight, old-fashioned roses and lychees) and taste. Lovely, rich and delicious – needs to be chilled.

Widely available

2007 Crawford Farm Gewürztraminer Riesling

$20–22 ☆☆☆ Screwcap

The combo of gewürztraminer with riesling is unusual since both grapes are so expressive in their own right. That said, this wine works in a clean, fresh, intensely aromatic way. Drink with Moroccan flavours – or anything with cumin, which tastes great with gewürztraminer, which is to the fore in this wine.

Widely available or www.crawfordfarm.co.nz

2007 Crossroads Hawke's Bay Gewürztraminer

$16–17 ☆☆☆ Screwcap

A very light Hawke's Bay gewürztraminer – fresh, citrusy and light. Good for everyday drinking during the summer.

Widely available

2007 Forrest Estate Marlborough Gewürztraminer

$19–20 ☆☆☆☆ Screwcap

Like fresh, intense-tasting Turkish delight, this delicious gewürztraminer is completely beguiling. One sip leads you onto another and another – it's too good. Serve lightly chilled.

Widely available

2007 Greenhough Nelson Gewürztraminer

$23–24 ☆☆☆½ Screwcap

Nelson winemaker Andrew Greenhough makes small quantities of great-tasting wines from a range of aromatic grape varieties, including this beautifully floral gewürztraminer with its dry finish.

Specialist wine stores or email greenhough@clear.net.nz

2005 Huntaway Reserve Gisborne Gewürztraminer

$18–20 ☆☆☆½ Screwcap

Gisborne has been home to many of New Zealand's best-ever gewürztraminers, and this spicy, fresh, old-fashioned rose-petal-flavoured wine is one of them. It's light in body but beautiful chilled for that first glass of the night.

Widely available

2007 Kaikoura Marlborough Gewürztraminer

$17–19 ☆☆☆½ Screwcap

The first whiff of this southern gewürztraminer is stunning: all Turkish delight and old-fashioned roses in aroma. It's a light, dryish white; serve cool on a beach on a sunny day.

Specialist wine stores or www.kaikourawinery.co.nz

2007 Kim Crawford Gisborne Gewürztraminer

$19–20 ☆☆☆ Screwcap

Its high-profile name, great packaging and consistent wine quality mean the Kim Crawford range of wines is synonymous with good value. This North Island gewürztraminer is a light but fresh and clean white wine – aromatic but dry on the finish.

Widely available or www.kimcrawfordwines.co.nz

2007 Maimai Creek Hawke's Bay Gewürztraminer

$19–20 ☆☆☆½ Screwcap

Reminds me instantly of old-fashioned red roses and their intense but soft perfume. This is another reminder of New Zealand's strong potential with gewürztraminer – its spicy, rose flavours and perfume lead into a fresh, light-bodied white. Good with pistachios or your favourite salted nuts as a pre-dinner wine.

Online at www.maimaicreek.co.nz

2007 Montana Patutahi McLoughlin Block Gewürztraminer

$24–25 ☆☆☆½ Screwcap

Almost exactly the same rave review as below applies to this unctuous, big, luscious Turkish-delight-tasting gewürztraminer from Gisborne. I love it, and I'm sure you will – especially served with salty pistachios as a foil for its off-dry character.

Widely available

Star gewürztraminer

2007 Montana Riverpoint Gisborne Matawhero Gewürztraminer

$24–25 ☆☆☆½ Screwcap

If you love gewürztraminer, look no further for a treat than this lovely, unctuous and weighty version from Gisborne's Matawhero vineyard – which has long been home to some of this country's best 'gewurz'.

Widely available

2007 Mystery Creek Gewürztraminer $15–17 ☆☆☆½ Screwcap

This is a light, fresh white made from one of the most recognisable grapes around: highly perfumed gewürztraminer. Its aromas are all of Turkish delight and old-fashioned rose petals. This wine is relatively light in flavour but served chilled it's refreshing either late in the day or late at night when you're reviving.

Online at www.mysterycreekwines.com or email sales@atomdrinks.com

2007 Saints Gisborne Gewürztraminer $16–18 ☆☆☆½ Screwcap

Turkish delight, old-fashioned red roses, or a big squishy home-made marshmallow? Whichever way you look at gewürztraminer, Gisborne makes some of New Zealand's best versions. This spicy, light, clean 'gewurz' from Gisborne is one of them, offering intense aromas at an affordable price. Very good value.

Widely available

2007 Taylors Adelaide Hills Gewürztraminer

$18–20 ☆☆☆½ Screwcap

Love this cool, crisp gewürztraminer from Australia's Adelaide Hills wine region. It's true to type, with luscious Turkish-delight flavours and voluptuous body.

Widely available

2007 Villa Maria Private Bin East Coast Gewürztraminer

$24–25 ☆☆☆½ Screwcap

Like most New Zealand gewürztraminers, this North Island wine promises lots of everything on its luscious, old-fashioned rose-petal nose. That said, it's clean, fresh and modern in style. A good aperitif wine style to drink pre-dinner.

Widely available

2007 Waimea Nelson Gewürztraminer $21–22 ☆☆☆½ Screwcap

Thank goodness for gewürztraminer. It might be one of the most forgotten grapes and wines around, but it's also one of the easiest to recognise – and most alluring to drink, lightly chilled, on a hot summer's day. Buy some fresh salted pistachios to enjoy with this.

Specialist wine stores or www.waimeaestates.co.nz

2006 Willm Reserve Gewürztraminer $24–25 ☆☆☆½

Serve this wine lightly chilled to best enjoy its luscious, succulent Turkish delight taste-alike qualities.

Specialist wine stores

Grillo

'Grill-o'

No one is entirely sure where the grillo grape originated, but today it hangs out mostly in vineyards in Sicily and in Puglia at the 'heel' of the Italian 'boot'. It was once the base of Marsala. Also known as riddu, this white grape can withstand high temperatures and still retain the lively freshness that characterises good grillo. There may only be one grillo in this chapter but it's worth seeking out – and delivers fantastic value for money. Surprise yourself . . .

2007 La Mura Grillo Sicilia $14–16 ☆☆☆☆ Screwcap

Talk about fantastic value for money. This dry, almost salty-tasting Sicilian white wine instantly conjures up great seafood for me – and when it's Bluff oyster season in New Zealand, enjoy your next lot with this lovely white wine.

🛒 Specialist wine stores or for stockists contact Prodotti d'Italia, phone (09) 276 7140 or www.pdi.co.nz

Grüner veltliner

'Grooner velt-leener'

Grüner veltliner is Austria's indigenous white grape, which makes light-bodied, floral and soft white wines – mostly in Austria, with slow but steadily increasing experimentation in other countries too.

2006 Salomon Undhof Hochterrassen Grüner Veltliner

$23–24 ☆☆☆½ Screwcap

Wow! Not only do we have a grüner veltliner in New Zealand, but to get one at this price and with a screwcap . . . that's what I call progress. This wine is a distinctively aromatic but dry white with a light to medium body and lots of flavour interest. A must-try for white-wine lovers.

🛒 Specialist wine stores

Italian whites

These white wines do not obviously fall into other, better-known categories and are made from grape varieties that are not well known in this country – which is all the more reason to get to know these fresh white wines.

2006 Cecchi Orvieto $19–20 ☆☆☆

This is a very light, simple Italian white wine with hints of nutty aromas and flavours. Better with food than without.

Glengarry stores in the North Island and specialist wine stores nationwide

2006 Piccini Orvieto Classico $14–15 ☆☆☆½

Another light Italian white; this one is simple, clean and fresh – good with food or on a sunny day at the beach. Ideal for summer drinking.

Mostly restaurants or for stockists contact Prodotti d'Italia, phone (09) 276 7140 or www.pdi.co.nz

Moscato/muscat

'Mos-cart-o' or 'mus-cat'

The word moscato is Italian for muscat, and there are several variations on this often overlooked grape variety. Its prime appeal lies in its spicy, orange rind and floral aromas, which always translate through to the same flavours in the wine.

The best-known variations of moscato include moscadello (a local version or clone of the grape grown around Montalcino in Italy, according to Jancis Robinson's *Guide to Wine Grapes*); moscatel (Spanish); moscatel de Austria (mostly grown in Chile to make spirit); moscatel rosada (Argentina); moscato bianco; moscato di Alexandria; and moscaphilero. For all that, the most famous expression of muscat and (arguably) its greatest is in French dessert wines.

Muscat grapes were described by Pliny the Elder as *uva apiana*, which means 'grape of bees' because of the aromatic appeal they have to bees.

2007 Brown Brothers Moscato $15–16 ☆☆☆½

How could you not like this wine? Provided you serve it chilled, that is. The low alcohol (5.5 per cent) makes it the perfect daytime drink: refreshing, crisp (so long as it is chilled) and deliciously aromatic – even ever so slightly fizzy. It is made from the muscat grape.

🛒 Widely available

Other whites

2007 Esk Valley Hawke's Bay Chenin Blanc

$20–21 ☆☆☆☆ Screwcap

Remember chenin blanc? Whether your answer is yes or no, this is a wine you should definitely reacquaint yourself with – appley, dry as a bone and incredibly refreshing, it's a fantastic New Zealand white wine.

Widely available

2007 Piccini Albus $15–16 ☆☆☆½

Albus is the Latin word for 'white', and while this wine might have stiff competition from New Zealand's vast stable of white wines, it is a soft and pretty Tuscan white that tastes great mid to late afternoon. The grapes are malvasia and chardonnay, which combine to make a bright, fresh, off-dry white.

Supermarkets and wine stores or for stockists contact Prodotti d'Italia, phone (09) 276 7140 or www.pdi.co.nz

Piccini Bianco Sicilia $13–14 ☆☆☆

A simple, new-wave Sicilian white wine (non-vintage) made from three different grapes – cataratto, inzola and chardonnay – to produce a soft, light and smooth wine.

For stockists contact Prodotti d'Italia, phone (09) 276 7140 or www.pdi.co.nz

Pinot blanc

'Pee-no blonk'

2007 Clayridge Vineyards Pinot Blanc $22–23 ☆☆☆☆ Screwcap

A fabulous white wine. Not only do you hardly ever find pinot blanc, but it's even rarer to come across one as delicious as this aromatic, floral Marlborough version. Chill and drink in summer. Fantastic stuff.

Specialist wine stores or www.clayridge.net.nz

Pinot gris

'Pee-no gree'

'We could bottle water and slap the label pinot gris on it and it would still sell like hotcakes,' said a well-known Gisborne winemaker, who understandably did not want to be quoted on the record. He went on to say that most of the winemakers he knew found the pinot gris phenomenon difficult to understand when most of them were producing more characterful-tasting wines from chardonnay, gewürztraminer and sauvignon blanc grapes.

Pinot gris is the best-known mutant grape variety of pinot noir, which mutates easily to other lesser-known varieties such as pinot blanc and a never-ending number of clonal variations of itself. It is known as pinot grigio in Italy, where it is usually vinified to be bone dry, but the best examples most often come from Alsace, France.

In 2005 pinot gris was the seventh most-planted grape in this country, with 462 hectares grown nationwide – more than 20 times the amount planted in 1996, when just 21 hectares were in the ground. This year pinot gris is poised to overtake riesling in plantings – and in popularity. It is currently all the rage compared with riesling's languishing reputation and misunderstood character, but that's another story . . .

For all its popularity, pinot gris in New Zealand is still very much a work in progress. There is not one but several styles, for a start. Under $15, it is pretty difficult to find any defined varietal character or taste, but as a white that is simple and easy to enjoy, pinot gris is the wine of the moment.

It is not that good pinot gris is impossible to find, but in New Zealand, to date, most of the wine made from this white grape variety is so innocuous that it virtually demands to have a little residual sugar left in it to enhance its very light flavours.

Star pinot gris

2007 Clayridge Marlborough Pinot Gris

$24–25 ☆☆☆☆

2007 Ata Rangi Martinborough Pinot Gris $24–25 ☆☆☆ Screwcap

Light and simple Kiwi pinot gris from this small Martinborough winery.

Specialist wine stores or www.atarangi.co.nz

2007 Aurum Pinot Gris $18–20 ☆☆☆½ Screwcap

Central Otago is good for lots of things – including this spicy, fresh, textural and even relatively weighty pinot gris. Drink a glass or two in the sunshine this summer.

Specialist wine stores or www.aurumwines.com

2006 Bolla Pinot Grigio $17–18 ☆☆☆

Like most pinot grigio, this is a dry white with a relatively simple, light body and style. Drink with food to get the best out of this Italian white.

Glengarry stores in the North Island and specialist wine stores nationwide

2006 Bollini Pinot Grigio Trentino $24–25 ☆☆☆ Screwcap

The wine world is changing – this Italian pinot grigio is sealed with a screwcap. The wine itself is drier by far than most Kiwi versions, and although it is light, I prefer its more food-friendly qualities. Drink with a seafood entrée.

Specialist wine stores

2007 Camshorn Glenmark Gravels Pinot Gris

$24–25 ☆☆☆½ Screwcap

North Canterbury is home to great riesling but few pinot gris, bar this and a handful of others. This is a bright, fresh and lively wine from one of the most promising wine regions in New Zealand.

🛒 Specialist wine stores

2007 Canaletto Pinot Grigio $16–18 ☆☆☆ Screwcap

Labelled 'autentico Italiano', this pinot grigio (the same wine as pinot gris, just a different name) is light and dry in style. It's good served lightly chilled (rather than chilled to within an inch of its life) with salty nuts and soft cheese.

🛒 Wine stores or for stockists contact Prodotti d'Italia, phone (09) 276 7140 or www.pdi.co.nz

2007 Cape Campbell Marlborough Pinot Gris

$18–19 ☆☆☆ Screwcap

Simple, light, fresh and off-dry – this is a decent lunchtime drop, nothing more.

🛒 Liquor stores or www.capecampbell.co.nz

2007 Carrick Central Otago Pinot Gris $23–24 ☆☆☆½ Screwcap

If one region in New Zealand has the ability to make pinot gris that is distinctively different from the rest, Central Otago has to be that place. This wine has a nervy edge: fresh, vibrant acids couple with hints of pear juice and a long finish.

🛒 Specialist wine stores or www.carrick.co.nz

2005 Cavallina Sicilia Pinot Grigio $14–15 ☆☆☆ Screwcap

Very light, fresh pinot grigio from Sicily. An everyday white.

🛒 La Barrique, Auckland, phone (09) 638 5000 or 524 6666, and Sovrano, Auckland, phone (09) 271 5969

2007 Church Road Hawke's Bay Pinot Gris $20–22 ☆☆☆ Screwcap

Light, fresh, simple pinot gris with hints of pear juice and spice in taste. Chill lightly and enjoy in summer.

Widely available

Star pinot gris

2007 Clayridge Marlborough Pinot Gris

$24–25 ☆☆☆☆ Screwcap

Four stars for a pinot gris? This wine wows with body, weight, texture and energetic zest. I really enjoy the taste – for a couple of glasses. Serve chilled.

Specialist wine stores or www.clayridge.net.nz

2007 Commissioner's Block Pinot Grigio $15–16 ☆☆☆½ Screwcap

This is a lovely, light Australian pinot grigio – clean, fresh and slightly spicy.

Liquor stores or www.neqtarwines.com.au

2007 Corazón SV Pinot Gris Marlborough $24–25 ☆☆☆½

Soft and smooth, this is one of the best pinot gris in the book this year, made by Auckland-based winemaker Shayne Cox. The word 'corazón' is Spanish for 'heart'.

Specialist wine stores or www.corazonwines.co.nz

2007 Corbans Gisborne Pinot Gris $14–15 ☆☆☆½ Screwcap

Finally . . . a good-value pinot gris at this low, low price. This wine is a significant improvement on last year's version under the same label. It is a simple white but has more weight than many that cost a lot more.

Widely available

2007 Corbans Private Bin Hawke's Bay Pinot Gris

$21–23 ☆☆☆½ Screwcap

This off-dry, aromatically spicy pinot gris is one of the best-value wines of its type under $20 in this wine guide. Soft in mouthfeel and body with light fruit flavours, it's an everyday white.

Widely available

2006 Crawford Farm Pinot Gris Chardonnay

$20–22 ☆☆☆ Screwcap

An unusual blend of pinot gris and chardonnay, and made for everyday drinking. It's just off-dry, clean and fresh – simple but reliable.

Widely available

2007 Distant Land Pinot Gris $19–20 ☆☆☆½ Screwcap

As pinot gris go, this is a lovely one – fresh, soft and lightly spicy. Its off-dry style adds appeal.

Specialist wine stores or www.distantland.co.nz

2007 Drylands Marlborough Pinot Gris $19–20 ☆☆☆ Screwcap

Light, fresh, crisp but off-dry in style, which accounts for its easy drinking appeal. Definitely more of a daytime wine.

Widely available

2007 Esk Valley Hawke's Bay Pinot Gris $23–24 ☆☆☆½ Screwcap

One of the tastiest pinot gris in the guide this year, driven by a clean, light freshness with hints of grapey, fruit-salad flavours and a dry-ish finish.

Widely available

2007 Fairhall Downs Pinot Gris $25 ☆☆☆ Screwcap

Everyone in the wine biz has their own label, and this one is the baby of the Smith and Small families in Marlborough. Their pinot gris is a fresh, zesty southern wine with lemon overtones – good for lunch with seafood.

🛒 Specialist wine stores or www.fairhalldowns.co.nz

2007 Forrest Estate Pinot Gris $19–20 ☆☆☆½ Screwcap

Luscious and easy to like, so long as it's lightly chilled, since this wine is most definitely made in an off-dry style. Easy to enjoy – better with salty nibbles than without.

🛒 Widely available

2007 Goldridge Estate Matakana Pinot Gris $14–16 ☆☆☆ Screwcap

Fresh and clean but off-dry and simple. Like most pinot gris, this is an everyday wine – the emphasis being firmly on the 'day' part of that. Ideal for light lunchtime drinking.

🛒 Specialist wine stores

2007 Goldridge Estate Matakana Premium Reserve Pinot Gris $18–20 ☆☆☆½ Screwcap

Full-bodied, off-dry white made from pinot gris. This is a soft, simple wine with fresh pear flavours – a reliably simple daytime drink.

🛒 Specialist wine stores

2007 Grove Mill Marlborough Pinot Gris $19–20 ☆☆☆½ Screwcap

Grove Mill is not only a very good Marlborough producer of high-quality aromatic wines (think riesling, sauvignon blanc and this pinot gris), but it's also the country's first carbon-zero winery. This is an off-dry, easy-to-drink daytime wine.

🛒 Widely available

2007 Isabel Marlborough Pinot Gris $20–21 ☆☆☆½ Screwcap

What a refreshing taste – not only the wine but the fact that a Marlborough pinot gris made in reasonable quantities has plenty of flavour! I like the fresh, dry pear aromas and taste here. It's good value.

Liquor stores and specialist wine stores or www.isabelestate.com

2007 Kaituna Valley Canterbury Pinot Gris

$18–20 ☆☆☆½ Screwcap

For an everyday white wine, this southern Kiwi pinot gris offers decent value for money because of its firm, linear acids – these add structure and interest in the mouth to the relatively simple flavours of pinot gris.

Liquor stores and specialist wine stores

2007 Kaituna Valley Marlborough Pinot Gris

$18–20 ☆☆☆ Screwcap

This is a pretty simple everyday pinot gris; not as tasty as the same-label wine made with grapes grown in Canterbury (see above).

Liquor stores and specialist wine stores

2007 Kim Crawford Pinot Gris $18–20 ☆☆☆½ Screwcap

If you're a fan of fresh, fleshy white pears, then you'll like this Kiwi pinot gris from big-name winery Kim Crawford Wines. It's fresh, light and nicely balanced – only just off-dry.

Widely available

2007 Lake Chalice Marlborough Eyrie Vineyard Pinot Gris

$18–20 ☆☆☆ Screwcap

Light, bright and fresh but a simple everyday white wine. Enjoy lightly chilled.

Widely available

2007 Lonestone Marlborough Pinot Gris

$20 ☆☆☆½ Screwcap

The popularity of pinot gris continues to climb to new heights, in New Zealand and around the world. This Marlborough pinot gris is a clean, fresh, fruit-driven version with more body than many.

🛒 Specialist wine stores or contact Bennett & Deller for stockists near you, phone (09) 378 9463

2007 Maven Marlborough Pinot Gris

$17–18 ☆☆☆½ Screwcap

For easy daytime drinking, this wine is light, fresh and just the right medicine. Serve lightly chilled to tame down its just off-dry edge.

🛒 Specialist wine stores

2007 Moana Park Dartmoor Valley Pinot Gris

$15–16 ☆☆☆ Screwcap

This is a lively but simple white made with grapes grown in the relatively cool climate of the Dartmoor Valley in Hawke's Bay. Good for a party or beach BBQ.

🛒 Specialist wine stores or www.moanapark.co.nz

2007 Montana Hawke's Bay Pinot Gris $14–15 ☆☆☆ Screwcap

Simple everyday pinot gris; passable if chilled lightly and enjoyed during the daytime. A great beach wine.

🛒 Widely available

2007 Mud House Gisborne Pinot Gris $19–20 ☆☆☆ Screwcap

Simple, light, fresh white wine – good for daytime drinking.

🛒 Specialist wine stores

2007 Mystery Creek Pinot Gris $16–17 ☆☆☆ Screwcap

Here's a light, fresh white wine – definitely a lunch or late-afternoon drink with its off-dry, fruit-led flavours. Enjoy with food and chill lightly.

Specialist wine stores or www.mysterycreekwines.com

2007 Neudorf Brightwater Pinot Gris $19–20 ☆☆☆½ Screwcap

One of the best Kiwi pinot gris each year; fresh, bright and deliciously balanced. Drink lightly chilled in summer.

Specialist wine stores or www.neudorf.co.nz

2007 Pasqua Night Harvest Pinot Grigio $16–17 ☆☆☆

A simple, light Italian pinot grigio with slightly spicy flavours. Serve lightly chilled with nibbles.

Glengarry stores in the North Island and specialist wine stores nationwide

2007 Renato Nelson Pinot Gris $18–20 ☆☆☆ Screwcap

This everyday pinot gris is from a small Nelson winery, which you are more likely to know if you live in that region than elsewhere. It's a simple, average-quality white – more of a summertime wine.

Specialist wine stores or www.renatoestate.co.nz

2006 Ruffino Lumina Pinot Grigio $14–16 ☆☆☆ Screwcap

It's great to see European wines adopting screwcaps for their easy-drinking whites, such as this Italian pinot grigio (the same grape as pinot gris, by a different name). This is a light, simple white with a fresh, clean style. Drink at a BBQ or on the beach in summer.

Specialist wine stores

2007 Sacred Hill Marlborough Pinot Gris $19–20 ☆☆☆½ Screwcap

Lovely weighty, full-bodied pinot gris with lots going for it – textural might not mean much, but take a couple of sips of this almost bone-dry pinot gris and you'll see exactly what I mean. Good value.

🛒 Widely available

2007 Sanctuary Marlborough Pinot Gris $14–16 ☆☆☆ Screwcap

Simple, light, off-dry white – no more, no less.

🛒 Widely available

2007 Sileni Cellar Selection Pinot Gris Hawke's Bay
$19–20 ☆☆☆ Screwcap

Light, simple white for lunchtime drinking.

🛒 Liquor stores and specialist wine stores

2007 Southbank Estate East Coast Pinot Gris
$19–20 ☆☆☆ Screwcap

Like so many pinot gris from all over the world, this one is simple, soft and light. It's a definite daytime drink, nothing more.

🛒 Widely available

2007 Spinyback Pinot Gris $17–18 ☆☆☆ Screwcap

This is a light, fresh, good daytime wine from the Waimea Estates winery and best served chilled. Like most pinot gris, this is a simple white, but as it's sealed with a screwcap, it is also reliably good for summertime drinking.

🛒 Liquor stores or www.waimeaestates.co.nz

2007 Stoneleigh Marlborough Pinot Gris $17–18 ☆☆☆ Screwcap

This is a fresh, dryish white wine made from that grape of the moment – pinot gris. It has hints of spice but is otherwise simple. Best served chilled for lunchtime drinking.

🛒 Widely available

2007 Te Mania Nelson Pinot Gris $19–20 ☆☆☆ Screwcap

Very light, off-dry white that provides refreshing summertime drinking – just make sure to serve it chilled to best enjoy its aromatics and hint of sweetness in taste.

🛒 Specialist wine stores or www.temaniawines.co.nz

2006 Teviotdale Single Vineyard Pinot Gris

$19–20 ☆☆☆½ Screwcap

Like most Kiwi pinot gris, this one is noticeably off-dry in taste – and that's to add a little lift and flavour to the style. This is one of the best pinot gris made in New Zealand right now, due to the craftsmanship of seasoned winemaker Alan McCorkindale.

🛒 Specialist wine stores

2007 The Ned Pinot Gris $24–25 ☆☆☆ Screwcap

Winemaker Brent Marris' aim here was to make an Italian-styled pinot gris (aka pinot grigio – the Italian name for the same grape variety). To that end, this wine is nearly bone dry and has light pear flavours and a fresh, crisp style.

🛒 Widely available

2007 Thornbury Marlborough Pinot Gris $20–21 ☆☆☆½ Screwcap

This soft, light Marlborough pinot gris has fresh, clean, lightly fruity flavours going for it. The wine is just off-dry, making it good with antipasto at lunchtime on a hot day.

🛒 Widely available

2006 Thorn-Clarke Sandpiper Pinot Gris $20–21 ☆☆☆ Screwcap

Almost more a pinot grigio (usually drier) than a pinot gris, this Australian white wine is a good late-afternoon or first-course dinner party drop. Fresh, clean, and especially good with seafood.

Widely available

2007 Ti Point Pinot Gris $19–20 ☆☆☆ Screwcap

Medium-dry are words you rarely hear applied to white wine these days, but pinot gris like this fits that description well. Winemaker Tracy Haslam has made this pinot gris in a noticeably off-dry style to suit daytime drinking – so long as it's lightly chilled.

Glengarry stores and other specialist wine stores or www.tipoint.co.nz

2007 Tussock Nelson Pinot Gris $18–20 ☆☆☆ Screwcap

Firm fresh acids give appeal to this otherwise simple wine. Everyday drinking or take to the beach.

Liquor stores and specialist wine stores

2007 Vavasour Awatere Valley Pinot Gris
$18–20 ☆☆☆½ Screwcap

Vavasour is the oldest, best-known Awatere Valley winery and this is a beautifully aromatic, intense-tasting pinot gris with aromas and flavours of pear. Serve just lightly chilled, winter or summer.

Widely available

2007 Villa Maria East Coast Pinot Gris $17–18 ☆☆☆ Screwcap

Its light-pink colour comes from its relationship with the red grape pinot noir, and its soft, off-dry flavours make this wine easy to enjoy. Just be sure to chill lightly before drinking.

Widely available

2007 Villa Maria Taylors Pass Marlborough Pinot Gris

$19–20 ☆☆☆½ Screwcap

This light, fresh, clean Marlborough pinot gris is one of the best under $25 in New Zealand right now. With flavours of pears, white peaches and fresh white grapes, it's a good daytime wine.

Liquor stores and specialist wine stores

2007 Waimea Nelson Bolitho Pinot Gris $24–25 ☆☆☆½ Screwcap

Not to be confused with its little sibling (below), this Waimea Estates pinot gris is a more weighty wine to drink and a better match for food too, especially if it's fresh shellfish or baked fresh fish.

Liquor stores or www.waimeaestates.co.nz

2007 Waimea Nelson Pinot Gris $21–22 ☆☆☆ Screwcap

From the relatively big Nelson winery, Waimea Estates, comes this fresh, bright pinot gris. It's definitely flavour of the month with a growing number of wine drinkers, but its light, slightly aromatic style makes it more of a daytime than an evening wine. Serve lightly chilled.

Liquor stores or www.waimeaestates.co.nz

2007 Waipara Hills Equinox Waipara Pinot Gris

$19–20 ☆☆☆ Screwcap

Lovely, soft and light pinot gris – good value for money and a bright expression of this light grape variety.

Specialist wine stores

2007 White Rock Pinot Gris Hawke's Bay $20-21 ☆☆☆

Fresh, bright, white wine made from one of the most popular white grapes of the moment, pinot gris.

Specialist wine stores or www.craggyrange.com

2007 Wild South Marlborough Pinot Gris $17–18 ☆☆☆½ Screwcap

Even if you're a big fan of pinot gris already, this one definitely stands out, especially at the price. It has overt pear juice aromas and even some spicy, clove-like flavours – and a long finish. Serve lightly chilled during the day.

🛒 Specialist wine stores

2007 William Thomas Marlborough Pinot Gris $23–24 ☆☆☆

Fresh, zingy Marlborough pinot gris with soft mouthfeel and flavours. Drink lightly chilled with food.

🛒 Specialist wines stores or www.williamthomaswines.co.nz

2006 Willm Reserve Pinot Gris $24–25 ☆☆☆½

This Alsacien pinot gris from France is fresh, floral and spicy. It's a very light style of white wine, best suited to salty nuts, a light chilling and a hot day.

🛒 Specialist wine stores

2007 Woollaston Burke's Bank Pinot Gris $19–20 ☆☆☆ Screwcap

This Nelson-grown and -made pinot gris is off-dry, which adds a little weight and interest in the mid-palate, otherwise a simple everyday number.

🛒 Liquor stores and specialist wine stores

2007 Zilzie Pinot Grigio $18–19 ☆☆☆

Fresh, light, simple Australian pinot grigio. Chill and drink on your favourite beach during a hot summer's day.

🛒 Specialist wine stores

Riesling

'Rees-ling'

What is your least favourite white wine? If you say riesling I won't be surprised, but what takes many wine drinkers by surprise is hearing wine writers and winemakers say that they love this perennially unpopular grape.

It is the history of riesling rather than any current surge in its popularity that puts this grape among the great classics of the wine world. In the late nineteenth and early twentieth centuries the greatest German rieslings were as highly valued as the best French reds were at the time. Today, both the name and the expectations that lie behind the word 'riesling' confer a low-quality image for many wine drinkers.

The apprehension for many is based both on poor-quality versions and on many cheap and not-so-cheerful white wines made from inferior grape varieties but labelled as 'riesling'. The tide has turned again, however, and riesling producers in New World countries do a better job with the grape variety than they did a couple of decades ago.

Riesling will soon be overtaken by pinot gris in New Zealand's vineyards, but a little detail like numbers is not stopping some of this country's best winemakers from searching for the perfect Kiwi riesling. Watch this space!

The benchmark rieslings of the world come both from Alsace in northern France and from the Rhine and Mosel-Saar-Ruwer regions of Germany. The food eaten with riesling depends entirely on the style of wine – whether it is bone dry and higher in alcohol, or low in alcohol and slightly sweet in taste, or a dessert wine.

Star riesling

2006 Knappstein Clare Valley Hand Picked Riesling

$22–24 ☆☆☆☆½

2006 Allan Scott Marlborough Riesling $19–20 ☆☆☆½ Screwcap

Like most Marlborough rieslings, this one is seriously underrated – fresh, vibrant, intense and zingy. It's good drinking now, but will continue to develop classic aged-riesling flavours of citrus and honey. Good lightly chilled with your favourite salty nibbles.

Widely available

2007 Anchorage Classic Riesling Nelson $18–20 ☆☆☆½ Screwcap

Here's a riesling that shows just how fantastic this varietal can be – its flavours span the gamut of apple freshness and bright acids to a lingering, lime-tasting finish. I love it, and I'm sure it's going to find a large fan club.

Specialist wine stores or www.anchoragewines.co.nz

2006 Aurum Central Otago Riesling $19–20 ☆☆☆½ Screwcap

This Central Otago riesling is a clean, fresh and very dry wine – great with nibbles on a summer day.

Specialist wine stores

2007 Blackenbrook Nelson Riesling $22–23 ☆☆☆½ Screwcap

It might be this winery's chardonnay and sauvignon blanc that are adorned – nay, smothered – in medal stickers, but I love this type of riesling. At first it seems light and citrusy, but there is such intense freshness and a long finish that it is the wine I want to drink around summer BBQs.

Specialist wine stores in Nelson and Auckland, or www.blackenbrook.co.nz

2006 Camshorn Waipara Salix Clays Dry Riesling

$24–25 ☆☆☆☆ Screwcap

A brave new dry wine from riesling fanatic and viticulturist Martin Tillard. This is a weighty wine with lots of time on its side – and good drinking now. It has a long, thought-provoking finish (riesling fans know what I mean).

Specialist wine stores

2007 Clayridge Marlborough Wild Riesling

$24–25 ☆☆☆☆ Screwcap

Is it possible to be too fresh, too light and too intense all in one fell swoop? It's rieslings such as this that really hit the spot of wine lovers who have fallen for the charms of the riesling grape. At just 10.5 per cent alcohol, it's easy on the body – as well as being delicious on the tastebuds.

Specialist wine stores or www.clayridge.net.nz

2006 Clifford Bay Marlborough Riesling

$19–20 ☆☆☆☆ Screwcap

Like most rieslings, this limey, appley, dry South Island version is wildly underrated. It's almost bone dry and much more refreshing and food-friendly than most as a result. I love it – hope you do too.

Specialist wine stores

2006 Corbans Waipara Riesling $14–15 ☆☆☆½ Screwcap

Like most Waipara rieslings, this one is a pure expression of this great grape – albeit at a low price. I like the limey dryness here; it's a very brave wine and great value.

Widely available

2006 Craggy Range Single Vineyard Riesling
$22–23 ☆☆☆½ Screwcap

Gorgeous Waipara riesling with light body, lime flavours and deliciously concentrated. Love it. Serve lightly chilled.

Specialist wine stores or www.craggyrange.com

2006 Drylands Marlborough Dry Riesling $19–20 ☆☆☆ Screwcap

Large-scale production doesn't sacrifice riesling's instantly recognisable hallmarks here – apple freshness and vibrancy in the glass. Good late-afternoon wine in summer.

Widely available

2007 Esk Valley Hawke's Bay Riesling $20–21 ☆☆☆½ Screwcap

Limes, green apples and fresh citrusy lemon flavours team up in this refreshing, dry riesling from Hawke's Bay. A lovely light, summer style.

Widely available

2006 Five Flax East Coast Riesling $10–12 ☆☆☆½ Screwcap

The words 'East Coast' on the label of this North Island riesling mean that the grapes were grown in a combination of regions. It's a light white but easily says 'riesling' on the palate, in an off-dry fashion. Good everyday drinking that offers a great introduction to riesling. Be sure to chill it lightly.

Widely available

2007 Forrest Estate Dry Riesling $19–20 ☆☆☆½ Screwcap

At the first sip this seems very light, but it's the dryness that is deceptive, leading into a lively, fresh, even slightly weighty palate. Very good.

Specialist wine stores or www.forrestwines.co.nz

2007 Forrest Estate Marlborough Riesling

$19–20 ☆☆☆☆ Screwcap

Like all of the rieslings from this big-name, well-established Marlborough winery, this one is screaming to be enjoyed lightly chilled with food. Fresh, clean, bright and incredibly long on flavour, its luscious apple and lime flavours never seem to finish. Great value for money.

🛒 Specialist wine stores or www.forrestwines.co.nz

2006 Forrest Estate The Doctor's Riesling $19–20 ☆☆☆☆

Utterly sensational riesling from Marlborough; its low alcohol content of less than 10 per cent adds to its lightness and take-you-by-surprise appeal. Love it.

🛒 Specialist wine stores or www.forrestwines.co.nz

2006 Gisselbrecht Riesling $21–22 ☆☆☆

This Alsacien riesling is a lively, fresh, but light everyday white wine. It's dry in style with a medium finish.

🛒 Glengarry stores in the North Island and specialist wine stores nationwide

2007 Grove Mill Marlborough Riesling

$18–20 ☆☆☆½ Screwcap

This is consistently one of Marlborough's best rieslings in this price range; fresh, clean and intensely citrusy with an off-dry finish.

🛒 Specialist wine stores and some supermarkets

2007 Hay Maker South Island Riesling $18–20 ☆☆☆

Like most South Island rieslings, this is a light-bodied wine, fresh, clean and full of lime flavours.

🛒 Specialist wine stores

2004 Hunter's Marlborough Riesling $19–20 ☆☆☆ Screwcap

Easy-drinking Marlborough riesling with developed, interesting flavours of preserved lemons and limes; ready to drink now. Serve lightly chilled with chips and dip.

Widely available or www.hunters.co.nz

2007 Hunter's Marlborough Riesling $18–20 ☆☆☆½ Screwcap

To describe this Marlborough riesling as luscious is to understate its appeal. Light but limey, with medium weight and a lingering and beguiling finish . . . this is great value.

Widely available

2007 Jacob's Creek Riesling $13–14 ☆☆☆½ Screwcap

It's light, it's limey and apple-like in flavour and it's a great price for an almost bone-dry tasting wine. This is a great place to start with riesling.

Widely available

2007 Kim Crawford Marlborough Dry Riesling
$19–20 ☆☆☆½ Screwcap

A consistent winner with riesling fans and newcomers to good riesling. This wine stands out for its intense flavour, freshness and the dry, food-friendly finish.

Widely available or www.kimcrawfordwines.co.nz

Star riesling

2006 Knappstein Clare Valley Hand Picked Riesling

$22–24 ☆☆☆☆½ Screwcap

Rare, zingy, deliciously good in every way — this wine starts out with an appealingly light and limey hint of sweetness, moving through to a bone-dry palate and lingering finish. It's an absolute stunner from Australia's Clare Valley – sensational even if it cost a lot more than this.

🛒 Specialist wine stores

2007 Konrad Marlborough Riesling $19–20 ☆☆☆½ Screwcap

If it needs to be said again, Kiwi riesling is one of the most underrated wines around – and this is no exception. Green apple and fresh lime flavours team up in each glass of this, offering loads of flavour – and good value too.

🛒 Specialist wine stores

2007 Lake Chalice Marlborough Riesling $18–20 ☆☆☆½ Screwcap

Is riesling the most undervalued wine on the planet? Or is it just wine fanatics like yours truly who think so? Whichever way it goes, this lovely, luscious Marlborough riesling will take your palate to new places – especially if it's served lightly chilled with salty pistachios.

🛒 Specialist wine stores or www.lakechalice.com

2006 Lawson's Dry Hills Marlborough Riesling

$20 ☆☆☆☆ Screwcap

If all New Zealand rieslings were as good as this, we'd have a massive riesling movement on our hands. Lovely, lively, lingering in flavour, and fresh as a daisy in taste. This is the perfect wine to begin the evening with, prior to moving onto reds. It's also the perfect wine to refresh your palate at the end of the night. Delicious.

🛒 Liquor stores and specialist wine stores or www.lawsonsdryhills.co.nz

2007 Maimai Creek Hawke's Bay Riesling $18–20 ☆☆☆☆ Screwcap

What is New Zealand's most undervalued white wine? Why, riesling of course. Lively, fresh, light bodied but at the same time intense in taste – if it sounds like a paradox, you only need a sip of this sensational white to begin to understand what good riesling is all about.

Online at www.maimaicreek.co.nz

2006 Main Divide Canterbury Riesling $19–20 ☆☆☆½ Screwcap

Some call it a second tier, others refer to it as a delineated brand, but the makers of this wine prefer to describe it as merely an alternative to their main Pegasus Bay range – the main alternative being its more accessible price. This is a luscious riesling – all limes, honey and drink-me-now deliciousness.

Widely available or www.maindivide.com

2007 Matua Regional Reserve Marlborough Riesling
$21–22 ☆☆☆ Screwcap

Dry-wine style with appealing lime flavours. Serve with barbecued prawns doused in fresh lime.

Widely available or email sales@matua.co.nz

2006 Mitchell Watervale Riesling $23–24 ☆☆☆☆ Screwcap

Awesome Australian riesling, and I'm not just saying that to use a little alliteration. This really is a lovely, bone-dry, pure riesling – a great expression of what Australia's Clare Valley can do with the world's greatest white grape variety. Lightly chill and serve with pan-fried prawns with garlic and lime, just to see how great it is.

Liquor stores and specialist wine stores

2006 Momo Marlborough Riesling $19–20 ☆☆☆½ Screwcap

This is always good; a bright, vibrant Marlborough riesling with piercing lime and apple intensity. What better wine to drink on a spring day in the sunshine at the beach?

🛒 Specialist wine stores

2006 Montana Reserve Waipara Riesling $14–15 ☆☆☆½ Screwcap

It's a nod to the future of good New Zealand riesling that the grapes in this wine were grown in Waipara, North Canterbury – home to some of the best Kiwi rieslings. Appley fresh but just off-dry in style, this wine feels almost bone dry. Very good value it is, too.

🛒 Widely available

2007 Montana South Island Riesling $14–16 ☆☆☆½ Screwcap

This South Island riesling is a big step up from previous vintages of the big 'M' – Montana's widely produced riesling. It's definitely off-dry in style but appley fresh, clean and with a pure limey flavour. Good for a couple of after-work glasses.

🛒 Widely available

2007 Mud House Waipara Riesling $19–20 ☆☆☆☆ Screwcap

Been bitten by the riesling bug yet? If not, a taste of this limey, dry riesling will have you rethinking the grape, the wine it makes and how food-friendly this is.

🛒 Liquor stores and specialist wine stores

2007 Murdoch James Blue Rock Riesling $20–21 ☆☆☆ Screwcap

Really good Martinborough riesling that is noticeably off-dry in style – which balances this wine beautifully. Make sure it's lightly chilled.

🛒 Specialist wine stores

2007 Murdoch James Two Islands Riesling $20–21 ☆☆☆ Screwcap

Light, simple riesling from Martinborough. Chill it and drink during the day.

Specialist wine stores

2007 Mystery Creek Gisborne Riesling $16–17 ☆☆☆ Screwcap

The Mystery Creek winery sources grapes from different regions to make good-value everyday drinking wines, such as this fresh green apple-tasting riesling. It's light, off-dry in a 'medium' (yes, that's tricky to define) style. Enjoy with salted nuts, which will match the slight hints of sweetness in the wine.

Specialist wine stores or www.mysterycreekwines.com

2006 Neudorf Brightwater Riesling $22–25 ☆☆☆☆ Screwcap

Brightwater is a small sub-region of Nelson and home to some of the best aromatic whites from the high-quality Neudorf Vineyards. This is sensational riesling – fresh, intense but light too, showing the potential of this undervalued grape variety.

Online at www.neudorf.co.nz

2004 Nottage Hill Hardys Riesling $9–10 ☆☆☆½ Screwcap

It may be a big-name, mass-produced, everyday white wine, but this Australian riesling is great value for money and incredibly tasty too. Light, fresh, limey and off-dry, it's excellent with Thai food.

Widely available

2007 Palliser Estate Martinborough Riesling
$19–20 ☆☆☆ Screwcap

Intensely fruity, fresh, grapefruity-citrusy riesling from Martinborough.

Specialist wine stores or www.palliser.co.nz

2007 Saint Clair Riesling $19–20 ☆☆☆ Screwcap

Fresh limes, green apples and bright grapefruit flavours shine through in this primary fruit-scented Marlborough riesling. It's a drink-me-now white. Chill lightly and enjoy in summer. Good value.

Widely available

2004 Sanctuary Marlborough Riesling

$16–17 ☆☆☆½ Screwcap

For those who love riesling, this is a lovely aged version of the stuff from New Zealand's largest wine region – Marlborough. Drink it lightly chilled, preferably mid-afternoon in the (dappled) sunshine.

Widely available

2003 Sandalford Western Australia Riesling

$19–20 ☆☆☆ Screwcap

Interesting dry riesling from Western Australia; drink with food rather than without as, at five years old now, this wine needs an accompaniment.

Liquor stores and specialist wine stores

2007 Selaks Marlborough Riesling $14–15 ☆☆☆½ Screwcap

Even at this price, riesling is one of the purest, most expressive wines around. This is a very light version – just like fresh limes in a glass. Good for summer at the beach.

Widely available

2007 Seresin Memento Riesling $19–20 ☆☆☆½ Screwcap

Riesling is always getting write-ups from its small club of fanatics, raving that it'll be the next big thing. Nothing could be further from the truth. Riesling is a wine that wine drinkers relegate to the realms of 'occasional drinking', but give it a try and you'll love its light, lemony flavours – and the low 11 per cent alcohol.

Specialist wine stores or www.seresin.co.nz

2007 Sileni The Don Hawke's Bay Riesling

$19–20 ☆☆☆ Screwcap

Fresh, bright Kiwi riesling with soft mouthfeel and light appley flavours. Lovely late-afternoon wine.

Liquor stores and selected supermarkets or www.sileni.co.nz

2007 Spring Creek Estate Marlborough Riesling

$18–20 ☆☆☆☆ Screwcap

This is my kind of riesling – luscious, intensely limey and utterly delicious. It walks a tightrope of intense flavour but seemingly light body with a lingering flavoursome finish.

Specialist wine stores or www.springcreekestate.co.nz

2007 Spy Valley Marlborough Riesling $19–20 ☆☆☆☆ Screwcap

If you thought the 2006 Spy Valley riesling was good, then pour yourself a glass of this sensational, almost bone-dry riesling. Zingy and fresh in taste, this is one stunning wine that will turn your head – and your tastebuds. Too drinkable.

Widely available

2007 St Hallett Eden Valley Riesling $19–20 ☆☆☆☆ Screwcap

Full of fresh lime, apple and even lightly spicy flavours, this is Eden Valley riesling at its best, offering incredibly good value for money as well as loads of flavour. Dry in style with a long finish – what more can you ask for?

Specialist wine stores

2007 Taylors Clare Valley Riesling $18–20 ☆☆☆½ Screwcap

It's the dry, limey character of this wine that's a dead giveaway to its Australian origin. Drink with fresh Thai green mango salad, which matches its aromatic green flavours well.

🛒 Widely available

2006 Te Mania Nelson Riesling $17–18 ☆☆☆ Screwcap

An everyday riesling from Nelson – medium bodied but lacks concentration and definition of flavour.

🛒 Specialist wine stores or www.temaniawines.co.nz

2007 Tohu Marlborough Riesling $18–19 ☆☆☆ Screwcap

This Marlborough riesling is full of green ginger and green apple flavours, in an off-dry style. A good everyday riesling, best served lightly chilled.

🛒 Specialist wine stores or www.tohuwines.co.nz

2006 Triplebank Awatere Valley Riesling
$22–23 ☆☆☆½ Screwcap

It's the almost audacious austerity of this Awatere Valley riesling that I love. At once fresh, clean, vibrant but also appley, limey and elusively hard to describe. It's one of Marlborough's best so-called 'commercially produced' rieslings today. Try it.

🛒 Widely available

2007 Two Sisters Riesling $22–23 ☆☆☆☆ Screwcap

Like many Central Otago rieslings, this wine makes you feel alive with its fresh, vibrant lime and apple flavours and a finish that lingers.

🛒 Specialist wine stores or www.twosisters.co.nz

2007 Vidal Marlborough Riesling $18–19 ☆☆☆☆ Screwcap

Here is an instantly loveable riesling, summer or winter. Fresh, zingy limes and apple flavours team up with beautifully balanced acids in a wine with an instant palate-cleansing style. Luscious and lovely.

Widely available

2007 Villa Maria Marlborough Riesling $17–18 ☆☆☆½ Screwcap

Everyday wine it may be, but this lively Marlborough riesling is one of the purest whites in the guide this year. Apples, limes and hints of honey through and through immediately give it away as a good-quality and good-value riesling.

Widely available

2006 Waimea Bolitho Riesling $21–22 ☆☆☆ Screwcap

This is a big, toasty Nelson riesling with surprising weight; it's medium to full bodied, making it better with food than on its own. Drink with light, creamy Indian curry.

Specialist wine stores or www.waimeaestates.co.nz

2007 Waimea Classic Riesling $17–18 ☆☆☆½ Screwcap

Instantly appealing riesling with bright, fresh, green apple and sweet lime aromas and flavours. This is an almost too-easy-to-like riesling – definitely off-dry in style, which adds to its appeal.

Specialist wine stores or www.waimeaestates.co.nz

2005 Waimea Nelson Dry Riesling $19–20 ☆☆☆½ Screwcap

Three years old and drinking beautifully. This is a dry riesling, but it's now that it's had a little bottle-aging time that it is drinking fantastically well – think liquid honey, ginger and jasmine flowers.

Specialist wine stores or www.waimeaestates.co.nz

2007 Waipara Hills Riesling $19–20 ☆☆☆½ Screwcap

Waipara, North Canterbury, is one of the most promising places in New Zealand for top-tasting riesling right now – the climate is brilliantly suited to this grape. This is a lively, fresh, dry-tasting white wine with green apple and lime flavours. Good value too.

🛒 Specialist wine stores and Glengarry stores in the North Island

2007 Wairau River Marlborough Riesling
$19–20 ☆☆☆☆ Screwcap

This wine makes me pinch myself – is it just me, or is this exceptionally good value? It over-delivers on flavour, hugely. Even non-riesling fans will get into the intense, zesty lime flavours here that lead through to a lingering dry finish that keeps going on and on . . . in all the best ways.

🛒 Widely available or www.wairauriverwines.co.nz

2006 Wild Earth Central Otago Riesling
$17–18 ☆☆☆½ Screwcap

Lively appley and lime aromas and flavours lead into a definitely off-dry but appealing daytime-style riesling. Shows that Central Otago has outstanding riesling potential – not that it's news to some of us. Love this style.

🛒 Specialist wine stores or www.wildearthwines.co.nz

2007 Woollaston Nelson Riesling $19–20 ☆☆☆☆ Screwcap

In all its incarnations, this zingy riesling is one of the best in New Zealand at this price. I love its bright flavours, its mid-palate weight and its lingering finish. Great value.

🛒 Specialist wine stores or www.woollaston.co.nz

Sauvignon blanc

'So-vin-yon blonk'

Sauvignon blanc is one of the most instantly recognisable white wines in the world and is also New Zealand's most widely produced and biggest export wine. Nearly 8000 hectares of sauvignon blanc are planted everywhere in this country from Northland to Central Otago but most widely in Marlborough, where the wine's most distinctive permutation comes from. Most grape varieties in New Zealand are expanding in area planted throughout the country's vineyards, but sauvignon blanc is growing faster proportionately.

It is this country's most planted grape and most recognisable wine, and is destined to stay that way. And while the British have been those most enamoured of Kiwi sauvignon blanc since its star first ascended in the 1970s and 1980s, the North Americans are now besotted with Kiwi savvy too, albeit in a softer, slightly more off-dry style than the Brits' favourites.

Star sauvignon blanc

2007 Mahi Marlborough Sauvignon Blanc

$19–20 ☆☆☆☆½

2007 Akarua Marlborough Sauvignon Blanc

$20–22 ☆☆☆½ Screwcap

A bright, tropical-fruit-flavoured sauvignon blanc made with grapes grown in Marlborough but from a Central Otago winery. Good drinking in summer.

Specialist wine stores or www.akarua.com

2007 Alana Estate Martinborough Sauvignon Blanc

$19–20 ☆☆☆½ Screwcap

Alana Estate is a relative newcomer to the Martinborough wine scene and with a newish winemaker at the helm, crafting appealing, luscious wines, such as this flinty, dry sauvignon blanc. It's good value.

🛒 Liquor stores and specialist wine stores

2007 Anchorage Nelson Sauvignon Blanc

$19–20 ☆☆☆½ Screwcap

South Island sauvignon blancs like this one are instantly recognisable, and it's definitely more of a Nelson style than a Marlborough one. Green, fresh and tangy in taste – it's also clean, bright and great for drinking while it's young.

🛒 Specialist wine stores or www.anchoragewines.co.nz

2007 Askerne Sauvignon Blanc $16–17 ☆☆☆½ Screwcap

Here's a sauvignon blanc with an almost full-bodied style, due to some of the wine being aged in oak. It's also made with Hawke's Bay grapes, which is a style departure for Kiwi savvies. Good value.

🛒 Specialist wine stores or www.askerne.co.nz

2007 Ata Rangi Martinborough Sauvignon Blanc

$22–23 ☆☆☆½ Screwcap

Small but perfectly formed are the words most usually used to describe Martinborough's tiny Ata Rangi winery – and the year that was 2007 was a tiny one for its production. Only small quantities of this lovely, fresh, light and pure-tasting sauvignon blanc remain in specialist wine stores. If you see it, snap it up and enjoy it with Bluff oysters or your favourite seafood.

🛒 Widely available

2007 Auntsfield Marlborough Long Cow Sauvignon Blanc

$22–23 ☆☆☆½ Screwcap

Big, bold and intensely fruity in flavour, this Marlborough sauvignon blanc has heaps of the wow factor that put Kiwi savvy in the mouths and minds of wine lovers around the world.

Widely available or www.auntsfield.co.nz

2007 Bach 22 Sauvignon Blanc $13–14 ☆☆☆ Screwcap

This is a very light but fresh and clean sauvignon blanc – perfect for beginners to wine because of the appeal its just off-dry flavours give to this wine.

Widely available

2007 Bel Echo Marlborough Sauvignon Blanc

$18–20 ☆☆☆ Screwcap

This is a light, fresh and very off-dry sauvignon blanc from New Zealand's largest wine region. Good value for everyday drinking, served just chilled to tame down its off-dry edge.

Specialist wine stores

2007 Benson Block Hawke's Bay Sauvignon Blanc

$16–18 ☆☆☆½ Screwcap

Like most Hawke's Bay sauvignon blancs today, this is softer and has a slightly fuller-bodied style than most Marlborough versions. At this price, it's still a light-ish white wine but clean, fresh and good everyday drinking for savvy fans.

Widely available

2007 Blackenbrook Nelson Sauvignon Blanc

$19–20 ☆☆☆☆ Screwcap

If you're wooed by stickers, this fresh young thing from Nelson will draw you right in. Lively and lighter in style than Marlborough sauvignon blancs, but every bit as flavoursome.

Specialist wine stores in Nelson and Auckland, or www.blackenbrook.co.nz

2007 Blicks Lane Marlborough Sauvignon Blanc

$18–19 ☆☆☆½ Screwcap

Lovely sauvignon blanc – a vibrant, fresh, good-value, new Marlborough wine brand.

Liquor stores and specialist wine stores

2007 Bouldevines Dogpoint Road Sauvignon Blanc

$19–20 ☆☆☆½ Screwcap

A bright, fresh and zingy sauvignon blanc from a good vintage in New Zealand's largest wine region – Marlborough.

Specialist wine stores

2007 Boundary Road Rapaura Road Marlborough Sauvignon Blanc

$22–23 ☆☆☆☆ Screwcap

Here's a Marlborough sauvignon blanc with everything a white-wine drinker wants – soft texture, sweet tropical fruit flavours and a clean, fresh, lingering finish. Very good value for money.

Widely available

2007 Cable Bay Marlborough Sauvignon Blanc

$18–20 ☆☆☆☆ Screwcap

Waiheke Island winemaker Neill Culley sources grapes from Marlborough to make this sensationally well-balanced sauvignon blanc. It's one of the best of the 2007s: bright, clean and full bodied, led by weight as well as fruit flavours. Love it.

Widely available or www.cablebayvineyards.co.nz

2007 Cape Campbell Marlborough Sauvignon Blanc

$18–19 ☆☆☆½ Screwcap

This wine is an instant winner with sauvignon blanc fans and anyone who enjoys intense, fresh, clean white wines. Packed with vibrant fruit flavours and a very long finish, it's great value at this price.

🛒 Liquor stores or www.capecampbell.co.nz

2007 Church Road Hawke's Bay Sauvignon Blanc

$23–24 ☆☆☆☆ Screwcap

Subtle, smooth and rounded sauvignon blanc is the order of the day in this lovely Hawke's Bay wine. It's great value for this style and price.

🛒 Widely available

2006 Churton Marlborough Sauvignon Blanc

$22–23 ☆☆☆☆

One of the few Kiwi sauvignon blancs still sealed with a cork, but due to Sam Weaver's good winemaking this is every bit the fresh, lively white we've all come to expect from Marlborough's most planted grape. It has a medium body and long finish, giving it food-friendly appeal.

🛒 Specialist wine stores

2007 Clayridge Vineyards Sauvignon Blanc

$20–21 ☆☆☆☆ Screwcap

Marlborough at its best in a good vintage by winemaker Mike Just, who owns this label. This wine is bright and fresh but also has lots of weight and body.

🛒 Specialist wine stores or www.clayridge.net.nz

2006 Clearview Estate Reserve Sauvignon Blanc

$23–25 ☆☆☆☆½ Screwcap

Here's a big, bold Marlborough sauvignon blanc with all the bells and whistles of a full-bodied white wine with aromatics too.

Specialist wine stores or www.clearviewestate.co.nz

2007 Clearview Estate Te Awanga Sauvignon Blanc

$19–20 ☆☆☆☆ Screwcap

It might be the little sibling to the big 'reserve' version (above), but this is a fresher, brighter style of wine. Yes, I know it's younger too – by a whole year – but this is a lighter, softer drink. It's medium bodied, rounded and allows sauvignon to shine.

Specialist wine stores or www.clearviewestate.co.nz

2007 Clifford Bay Estate Marlborough Sauvignon Blanc

$19–20 ☆☆☆☆ Screwcap

With its intense freshness and great vibrancy of flavour, how can you not rate this wine highly? This is a bright star on Kiwi sauvignon blanc's horizon.

Widely available

2007 Clos Marguerite Marlborough Sauvignon Blanc

$23–24 ☆☆☆☆ Screwcap

Think fresh, bright and intense, and you have the perfect description of this wine – from a small Marlborough winery that can definitely lay claim to the label 'boutique'. This is quality, no holds barred; full of flavour, zing and lift.

Specialist wine stores

2007 Coal Pit Cinquante Sauvignon Blanc

$24–25 ☆☆☆☆½ Screwcap

An intensely fresh newcomer from the deep south – Central

Otago. Coal Pit Vineyard is a family-owned winery and this is a bright, clean, gooseberry-tasting white wine.

Specialist wine stores or www.coalpitwine.com

2006 Cockatoo Ridge Sauvignon Blanc $12–13 ☆☆☆ Screwcap

It's light and less expressive than most Kiwi sauvignon blancs, but this wine is fresh and clean all the same – offering good value for everyday drinking.

Widely available

2007 Composite Sauvignon Blanc $24–25 ☆☆☆☆

If its word-free label isn't enough to make this newcomer to the Marlborough sauvignon scene a show-stealer, then its flavours are. Dry, full bodied, fruit driven with soft mouthfeel and lingering finish.

Specialist wine stores and restaurants or www.winegrowersofara.co.nz

2007 Condor's Forest Montana Marlborough Rapaura Sauvignon Blanc $20–22 ☆☆☆½ Screwcap

The classy-looking burgundy bottle that houses this Marlborough sauvignon blanc is part of an experimental range of wines under the trials of Montana Wines. This is a nicely balanced sauvignon blanc with bright, clean, herby flavours and intense melon fruit flavours.

Widely available

2007 Corbans Hawke's Bay Sauvignon Blanc $14–15 ☆☆☆ Screwcap

Light, fresh, soft sauvignon blanc from Hawke's Bay with less vibrant fruit than most Marlborough sauvignons. Very food-friendly and easy to enjoy for everyday drinking.

Widely available

2007 Crawford Farm Marlborough Sauvignon Blanc

$18–20 ☆☆☆☆ Screwcap

A newish label from the Kim Crawford wine stable, this is a deliciously intensely zingy sauvignon blanc from Marlborough. Packed with gooseberry, kiwifruit and fresh-cut grass aromas but with ripe fruit flavours. Lovely.

Widely available or www.crawfordfarm.co.nz

2007 Crossroads Marlborough Sauvignon Blanc

$19–20 ☆☆☆ Screwcap

This is a light Marlborough sauvignon blanc with crisp, fruit-driven flavours leaning towards gooseberry more than tropical tastes.

Widely available

2007 Culley Marlborough Sauvignon Blanc

$18–20 ☆☆☆☆ Screwcap

This Waiheke Island wine, from winemaker Neill Culley, is made with grapes grown in Marlborough. Soft, fleshy and with more body than most Marlborough sauvignons, this is a delicious, intense white wine that stands out from the crowd.

Specialist wine stores

2007 Daisy Rock Marlborough Sauvignon Blanc

$19–20 ☆☆☆½ Screwcap

Fresh as a daisy with bright, tropical fruit flavours – this is a modern wine from its label to its passionfruity aromas to the last, lingering fruity drop.

Widely available

2008 Dashwood Marlborough Sauvignon Blanc

$18–19 ☆☆☆☆ Screwcap

You've got to love this wine for its fantastic flavours, which straddle the best of Marlborough's two main grape-growing regions – the vast Wairau Plains and the cooler Awatere Valley. It's crisp, intense and fruit driven without being over the top in taste.

🛒 Widely available or www.vavasour.com

2007 Deakin Sauvignon Blanc $15–16 ☆☆☆ Screwcap

Light, simple but fresh sauvignon blanc from Australia. It's a vastly simpler wine than its Kiwi counterparts but good everyday drinking served chilled.

🛒 Glengarry stores in the North Island and specialist wine stores nationwide

2007 Dog Point Marlborough Sauvignon Blanc
$23–24 ☆☆☆☆ Screwcap

Gorgeous sauvignon blanc with full-bodied style leading the way. It has lively, fresh, zesty flavours too, but is devoid of over-the-top grassiness. Love it.

🛒 Specialist wine stores or email info@dogpoint.co.nz

2007 Drylands Marlborough Sauvignon Blanc
$19–20 ☆☆☆½ Screwcap

Intense Marlborough savvy, with intense kiwifruit and gooseberry flavours. This is exactly the style of sauvignon blanc that has put New Zealand on the world's wine map in such a positive fashion.

🛒 Widely available

2007 Esk Valley Hawke's Bay Sauvignon Blanc
$20–21 ☆☆☆½ Screwcap

If you're a fan of Marlborough sauvignon blanc, then here is a gorgeously subtle alternative from Hawke's Bay. Slightly more tropical but dry in flavour, this is a more food-friendly and food-focused wine, with its soft, rounded body and flavours.

🛒 Widely available

2007 Fairhall Downs Sauvignon Blanc $19–20 ☆☆☆½ Screwcap

Here is a wine to wake you up. Like many 2007 Kiwi sauvignon blancs, it's bright, green and zesty in flavour. Great for lunchtime at the weekend when you want a fresh, clean, dry white.

Specialist wine stores or www.fairhalldowns.co.nz

2007 Five Flax Sauvignon Blanc $10–12 ☆☆☆ Screwcap

A good beginner's white wine – fresh, light and off-dry in style. Make sure it's served lightly chilled.

Widely available

2007 Forrest Estate Marlborough Sauvignon Blanc

$19–20 ☆☆☆½ Screwcap

From one of Marlborough's best-known, most established wineries – a bright, fresh, well-balanced sauvignon blanc that straddles new-wave tropical flavours with old-style gooseberry and kiwifruit tastes. Good value.

Widely available or www.forrestwines.co.nz

2007 Framingham Marlborough Sauvignon Blanc

$19–20 ☆☆☆½ Screwcap

Fresh, tropical fruit aromas couple with sweet mango and passionfruit flavours to make a fruit punch of a summer white wine from New Zealand's most planted grape variety.

Widely available

2007 Freefall Marlborough Sauvignon Blanc

$19–20 ☆☆☆½ Screwcap

Here's a wine that instantly says 'Marlborough sauvignon blanc' – it's bright, light, intense and gooseberry tasting. The style is clean and fresh. Good everyday drinking.

Specialist wine stores

2007 Gladstone Vineyard 12,000 Miles Sauvignon Blanc

$18–20 ☆☆☆☆ Screwcap

Named after winery owner Christine Kernohan's long journey from Scotland to New Zealand, this fresh, bright sauvignon blanc may taste every bit like a zingy, edgy Marlborough wine, but it's actually from the Wairarapa. Deliciously fresh.

🛒 Specialist wine stores or www.gladstone.co.nz

2007 Gladstone Vineyard Wairarapa Sauvignon Blanc

$24–25 ☆☆☆☆ Screwcap

This wine is a big, bold, lush and fruity Wairarapa sauvignon blanc with lots of weight, a surprisingly full-bodied style and a long finish.

🛒 Specialist wine stores or www.gladstone.co.nz

2006 Goldridge Estate Marlborough Sauvignon Blanc

$15–16 ☆☆☆½ Screwcap

This two-year-old Marlborough sauvignon blanc is fresh, light and dry and ready to drink now – wonderful with smoked fish pie.

🛒 Specialist wine stores

2006 Goldridge Estate Reserve Marlborough Sauvignon Blanc

$18–19 ☆☆☆½ Screwcap

An impressive Marlborough sauvignon blanc with rich tropical fruit flavours and a full body. It's slightly off-dry, which adds immediate appeal. It's essential to chill this wine lightly before drinking. Enjoy with pan-fried scallops, capers and parsley.

🛒 Specialist wine stores

2007 Goldwater Marlborough Sauvignon Blanc

$18–20 ☆☆☆☆ Screwcap

Goldwater Estate sauvignon blanc is made with Marlborough-grown grapes and takes its name from its own founders, the Waiheke Island-based Goldwater family. It's consistently one of the most balanced, rounded and drinkable sauvignon blancs each year – and good value, too.

🛒 Widely available

2007 Greenhough Nelson Sauvignon Blanc

$20–21 ☆☆☆½ Screwcap

Winemaker Andrew Greenhough makes this Nelson sauvignon blanc in a drink-me-now style. It's a fresh, fruity and medium-bodied sauvignon blanc – great summertime drinking. Love that dry finish.

🛒 Specialist wine stores or email greenhough@clear.net.nz

2007 Grove Mill Marlborough Sauvignon Blanc

$19–20 ☆☆☆½ Screwcap

A bright and fresh Marlborough sauvignon blanc with vibrant zing and a long, refreshing dry finish.

🛒 Widely available

2007 Hay Maker Marlborough Sauvignon Blanc

$16–17 ☆☆☆☆ Screwcap

If the words vibrant, zingy, firm acids and fresh as a daisy don't mean anything to you yet, they sure will after a taste of this lively sauvignon blanc.

🛒 Specialist wine stores and liquor stores and some supermarkets

2007 Hesketh Hidden Garden Marlborough Sauvignon Blanc

$18–19 ☆☆☆☆ Screwcap

Just 2000 cases of this flinty, fresh and tropical Marlborough sauvignon blanc were made by Australian Jonathan Hesketh, who sources grapes from all over the world for his relatively new range of Hesketh wines. This is top wine at a good price.

🛒 Specialist wine stores

2007 Hunter's Marlborough Sauvignon Blanc

$19–20 ☆☆☆½ Screwcap

One of the catch-cries of Hunter's Wines is that they are food friendly, and this lively, fresh sauvignon blanc perfectly fits that bill. Drink with your favourite oysters, freshly shucked, or any type of seafood.

🛒 Widely available or www.hunters.co.nz

2007 Isabel Marlborough Sauvignon Blanc

$20–21 ☆☆☆☆ Screwcap

Deliciously good sauvignon blanc with weight, body and texture as well as vibrantly fresh flavours. Really good wine – it might be a couple of dollars more than you usually spend, but you won't regret it.

🛒 Liquor stores and specialist wine stores or www.isabelestate.com

2006 Jackson Estate Marlborough Sauvignon Blanc

$19–20 ☆☆☆☆ Screwcap

It's always reassuring to come across wines as good as this lively, weighty and fresh sauvignon blanc. Big, tropical and fruit-salady, without being over the top – what more could you want in a glass of Marlborough savvy for great summertime drinking?

🛒 Widely available

2007 Kaikoura Marlborough Sauvignon Blanc

$18–19 ☆☆☆ Screwcap

A very light-bodied, fresh Marlborough white. Drink during the day or late afternoon.

Specialist wine stores or www.kaikourawinery.co.nz

2007 Kaituna Valley Marlborough Sauvignon Blanc

$19–20 ☆☆☆☆ Screwcap

Wow! Talk about a zingy white wine. This sauvignon blanc is pure, unadulterated freshness with vibrant green kiwifruit flavours and a long, clean finish.

Liquor stores and specialist wine stores

2007 Kawarau Estate Sauvignon Blanc

$19–20 ☆☆☆½ Screwcap

It's not every day you come across a sauvignon blanc that is grown and made in Central Otago, and this one is a bright, clean wine with exuberant acids, making it ideal to drink with food rather than on its own. Team it up with your favourite fresh fish and you'll have a good match.

Specialist wine stores or www.kawarauestate.co.nz

2007 Kim Crawford Marlborough Sauvignon Blanc

$19–20 ☆☆☆☆ Screwcap

Tropical fruit seems to leap onto the tongue in every sip of this intoxicating, passionfruity white wine. It's great value for money.

Widely available

2007 Koha Marlborough Sauvignon Blanc

$12–13 ☆☆☆½ Screwcap

Light in colour, body and flavour, this simple, fresh Marlborough sauvignon blanc is a good-quality entry-level wine made from New Zealand's largest wine region. Good everyday drinking.

🛒 Online at www.blackmarket.co.nz

2007 Kono Marlborough Sauvignon Blanc

$16–17 ☆☆☆☆ Screwcap

It's not only the name that has a quintessentially Kiwi ring to it – this gorgeous zingy sauvignon blanc from 2007 is juicy, clean and has a long finish.

🛒 Widely available

2007 Konrad Marlborough Sauvignon Blanc

$16–17 ☆☆☆½ Screwcap

Like the vast number of Marlborough sauvignon blancs, this one offers a delightful zing in your glass – lots of nicely balanced, fresh, appley flavours with a lingering finish.

🛒 Specialist wine stores

2007 Lake Chalice Marlborough Sauvignon Blanc

$19–20 ☆☆☆☆ Screwcap

Here's an intensely zingy Marlborough sauvignon blanc with gooseberry and kiwifruit flavours – entirely fruit driven, and best to drink and enjoy while it's young.

🛒 Specialist wine stores or www.lakechalice.com

2007 Lawson's Dry Hills Marlborough Sauvignon Blanc

$20–21 ☆☆☆½ Screwcap

Tropical but light Marlborough wine with hints of passionfruit and pineapple aromas and flavours – medium body and length.

🛒 Widely available or www.lawsonsdryhills.co.nz

Star sauvignon blanc

2007 Mahi Marlborough Sauvignon Blanc

$19–20 ☆☆☆☆½ Screwcap

The snail on the label of this wine is a dead giveaway to winemaker Brian Bicknell's philosophy – that good things take time. He takes longer than usual to craft this full-bodied sauvignon blanc, with its smooth texture and flavours. It is a stellar wine in a brave, more subtle than usual Kiwi style.

Specialist wine stores or email sales@mahiwine.co.nz

2007 Maimai Hawke's Bay Sauvignon Blanc

$16–17 ☆☆☆½ Screwcap

Hawke's Bay sauvignon blancs are typically softer and rounder in character than their Marlborough siblings, and this wine is no exception. It is still recognisable as Kiwi white wine, with fresh, bright flavours and acids, making it a good with-food partner.

Online at www.maimaicreek.co.nz

2007 Main Divide Marlborough Sauvignon Blanc

$19–20 ☆☆☆½ Screwcap

From the skilled winemakers Matthew Donaldson and Lynette Hudson comes this fresh, vibrant and lingeringly flavoursome sauvignon blanc. Good value indeed.

Widely available or www.maindivide.com

2006 Main Divide Sauvignon Blanc $19–20 ☆☆☆½ Screwcap

The most affordable range of the Pegasus Bay wine range, made from grapes grown around the South Island – which definitely translates to the cool, crisp, green flavours in this wine.

Specialist wine stores or www.maindivide.com

2007 Martinborough Vineyard Sauvignon Blanc

$20–22 ☆☆☆½ Screwcap

Martinborough may be small and best known for its pinot noirs, but aromatic whites such as this are among the jewels in its winemaking crown. Fresh, vibrant and fruity, this wine also tastes dry and refreshing.

🛒 Specialist wine stores or www.martinborough-vineyard.co.nz

2007 Matahiwi Estate Wairarapa Sauvignon Blanc

$18–19 ☆☆☆☆ Screwcap

From Opaki in the Wairarapa comes this zingy sauvignon blanc. It's lighter in style than most savvies from Marlborough, with more linear, even limey fresh flavours.

🛒 Specialist wine stores or www.matahiwi.co.nz

2007 Matua Regional Reserve Marlborough Sauvignon Blanc

$21–22 ☆☆☆☆ Screwcap

Wow! Here's a wine with zing and intensity – it's instantly likeable, big and bold, but with a soft finish, making it a good contender for drinking with seafood.

🛒 Widely available or email sales@matua.co.nz

2007 Maven Marlborough Sauvignon Blanc

🛒 $18–20 ☆☆☆☆ Screwcap

It's not only the evocative, photographic label that draws me to this bottle of zingy Marlborough sauvignon blanc, but I must admit that it's a big drawcard. Talk about a great partner for scallops, capers and butter.

🛒 Specialist wine stores or www.mavenwines.co.nz

2008 Mission Estate Hawke's Bay Sauvignon Blanc

$16–18 ☆☆☆½ Screwcap

One of the first sauvignon blancs off the block from the 2008 vintage – a bright, fresh, soft Hawke's Bay white.

Widely available

2007 Mission Kawera Road Sauvignon Blanc

$18–20 ☆☆☆☆ Screwcap

Who says Hawke's Bay can't produce stunningly expressive, pure and focused sauvignon blanc? If those wine jargony turns of phrase don't do it for you, then the delicious intensity of this wine certainly will. It's great value and a real coup for Hawke's Bay winery, Mission Estate.

Widely available

2007 Mission Reserve Sauvignon Blanc $19–20 ☆☆☆½

It's rare to find a Kiwi sauvignon blanc without a screwcap these days, but this big, soft Hawke's Bay savvy seems to suit the softening effect of a cork. Less intense than most Marlborough sauvignons, this is a lively wine nonetheless – and good value.

Widely available

Monkey Bay Marlborough Sauvignon Blanc

$10–12 ☆☆☆ Screwcap

Simple, fresh, tutti-frutti-flavoured, non-vintage sauvignon blanc – a good entry-level, beginner's Kiwi white wine.

Widely available

2007 Montana Awatere Rail Bridge Sauvignon Blanc

$23–25 ☆☆☆☆ Screwcap

Expect to hear a lot more of the Awatere Valley, just south of Marlborough's vast Wairau Plains. Both areas are home to grapes in the region and the Awatere's vineyards are growing by the month. Wines such as this have more depth of flavour than most whites from Marlborough, giving an edge in quality and enjoyment factor.

Liquor stores and specialist wine stores or www.montana.co.nz

2007 Montana Brancott Festival Block Sauvignon Blanc

$22–24 ☆☆☆½ Screwcap

Experimental new Marlborough sauvignon blanc from one of the region's oldest vineyards. Rounded, medium bodied, fresh and vibrant, this is a lovely, luscious wine.

Widely available

2007 Mud House Marlborough Sauvignon Blanc

$19–20 ☆☆☆☆ Screwcap

Here's an intensely zingy Marlborough sauvignon blanc with great length of flavour. Drink with salty cashews or your favourite nuts and tasty cheese to provide a good contrast.

Liquor stores and specialist wine stores

2007 Mud House Swan Marlborough Sauvignon Blanc

$24–25 ☆☆☆☆½ Screwcap

Easily the best by far of a trio of wines from the Mud House winery, which is in Waipara, North Canterbury. The grapes from which this wine was made were grown in Marlborough, New Zealand's largest wine region.

Liquor stores and specialist wine stores

2006 Mystery Creek Reserve Sauvignon Blanc

$24–25 ☆☆☆½ Screwcap

Instantly tastes like a Marlborough sauvignon blanc, and a quick look at the back label confirms this. It has those prickly fresh acids and vibrant fruity style that define a Marlborough savvy. The finish is medium, but the screwcap allows the wine's inherent freshness to come out in every sip. Good value too.

Specialist wine stores or www.mysterycreekwines.com

2007 Nautilus Marlborough Sauvignon Blanc

$19–20 ☆☆☆☆ Screwcap

It's not just the evocative name, the fact that most Marlborough sauvignon blancs are distinctive, or that this wine has a little bottle age, it is simply that this is a lovely sauvignon blanc – fresh, bright and intensely fruity with a nervy edginess that makes it worth every cent.

Widely available

2006 Neudorf Sauvignon Blanc Nelson $22–25 ☆☆☆½

A super-textural, weighty, drink-young Nelson sauvignon blanc – a really good match with fresh seafood.

Neudorf Vineyards, phone (03) 543 2643 or www.neudorf.co.nz

2007 Nobilo Icon Marlborough Sauvignon Blanc $23–24 ☆☆☆½

A big, bold and fresh Marlborough sauvignon blanc with vibrant fruit flavours; good value too.

Widely available

2007 Nobilo Marlborough Sauvignon Blanc

$12–14 ☆☆☆½ Screwcap

This big-name wine brand delivers great value for money in this mass-produced Marlborough sauvignon blanc. It's fresh, clean and slightly off-dry in style.

Widely available

2007 O:TU Otuwhero Estates Marlborough Sauvignon Blanc
$19–20 ☆☆☆½ Screwcap

As its awards demonstrate, this is definitely a with-food wine. It's a light, fresh Marlborough sauvignon blanc with overt herb flavours and a clean style.

Specialist wine stores

2007 Palliser Estate Martinborough Sauvignon Blanc
$20–22 ☆☆☆☆ Screwcap

A winner with sauvignon blanc drinkers year after year; vibrant, punchy and fruit driven without being over the top. Lovely and clean with a lingering finish.

Specialist wine stores or www.palliser.co.nz

2007 Pencarrow Sauvignon Blanc $18–20 ☆☆☆☆ Screwcap

Like its big sibling, the Palliser Estate sauvignon blanc – also from this big-name Martinborough winery – this is a great savvy. Tropical and fresh but balanced beautifully with vibrant acids and a long finish. Very good stuff.

Specialist wine stores or www.palliser.co.nz

2007 Renato Nelson Sauvignon Blanc
$21–22 ☆☆☆½ Screwcap

Owned by Renat Nussbaumer, this little Nelson winery has a stunning outlook – and, more importantly, the wine in this bottle is a fresh, vibrant New Zealand sauvignon blanc. It's a slight style departure from Marlborough sauvignons, but still with that innate zing that defines Kiwi savvies.

Specialist wine stores or www.renatoestate.co.nz

2007 Richmond Plains Nelson Sauvignon Blanc

$18–19 ☆☆☆☆ Screwcap

Fresh, slightly off-dry and with luscious fruity flavours, this is one brilliant summertime wine – drink at the beach, lightly chilled.

Specialist wine stores or www.richmondplains.co.nz

2007 Rockburn Sauvignon Blanc $23 ☆☆☆½ Screwcap

Fresh, zingy and definitely a South Island sauvignon blanc with cool, crisp flavours erring on the kiwifruit and fresh-cut-grass taste profile.

Specialist wine stores or www.rockburn.co.nz

2007 Rongopai East Coast Sauvignon Blanc

$14–16 ☆☆☆ Screwcap

This East Coast sauvignon blanc, labelled with the New Zealand fern's koru, is a soft, light, simple white made from this country's most widely grown grape variety.

Liquor stores and selected supermarkets or www.rongopaiwines.co.nz

2006 Rose Tree Cottage Marlborough Sauvignon Blanc

$23–24 ☆☆☆ Screwcap

At two years old now, this light, clean and fresh Marlborough sauvignon blanc is softer than many with smooth acids, making it a good with-seafood white wine. Dry on the finish.

Widely available

2007 Russian Jack Sauvignon Blanc $19–20 ☆☆☆½

Aside from the great-looking label, this is a lovely, bright, fresh white made from New Zealand's most widely planted white grape – sauvignon blanc, grown in Martinborough. Gooseberry and passionfruit flavours combine in this tropical-tasting white.

Specialist wine stores or www.burntspur.co.nz

2007 Saints Hawke's Bay Sauvignon Blanc

$16–17 ☆☆☆½ Screwcap

Hard to believe this is a Hawke's Bay sauvignon blanc, it's got so much zing and tropical fruit taste. If you're after something with instant 'wow' factor to drink on a summer's day, this is it.

Widely available

2007 Sanctuary Marlborough Sauvignon Blanc

$12–14 ☆☆☆ Screwcap

Like many Marlborough sauvignon blancs these days, this one is noticeably off-dry in style – made for a light chilling and drinking on a summer day. Good value at this price.

Widely available or www.sanctuarywine.co.nz

2007 Selaks Marlborough Favourite Sauvignon Blanc

$14–15 ☆☆☆ Screwcap

This 'favourite' sauvignon blanc is a relative newcomer to the big-name Selaks stable of wines. It's light, clean and full of grassy, fresh flavours.

Widely available

2007 Selaks Marlborough Sauvignon Blanc

$14–15 ☆☆☆½ Screwcap

This is just the sauvignon blanc that made New Zealand white wines popular all over the wine-drinking world. This is light, off-dry and a good introduction to wines for those new to the vinous world.

Widely available

2007 Seven Terraces Marlborough Sauvignon Blanc

$18–20 ☆☆☆½ Screwcap

Here's an instantly likeable sauvignon blanc, full of fresh tropical fruit flavours with a slightly off-dry edge to it. Serve lightly chilled and enjoy as a top-notch summertime drop.

Specialist wine stores

2007 Sileni River Reach Hawke's Bay Sauvignon Blanc

$21–22 ☆☆☆½ Screwcap

This Hawke's Bay sauvignon blanc is a real style departure from most New Zealand savvies, which usually come from Marlborough. Softer in acids and mouthfeel, still vibrantly fruity and with rounded body, it is a high-quality sauvignon for special-treat drinking.

Specialist wine stores

2007 Sileni The Straits Marlborough Sauvignon Blanc

$24–25 ☆☆☆½ Screwcap

Instantly and intensely Marlborough sauvignon blanc, from the first whiff to the last, lingering sip. This is a gooseberry, kiwifruit and slightly grassy style of white – good daytime wine with fresh fish.

Specialist wine stores

2007 Southbank Estate Marlborough Sauvignon Blanc

$19–20 ☆☆☆ Screwcap

Fresh, vibrant sauvignon blanc for everyday drinking – big in flavour but light in body. A good everyday wine.

Online at www.southbankestate.com

2007 Spinyback Nelson Sauvignon Blanc $14–15 ☆☆☆½ Screwcap

Talk about a flavour difference from Marlborough sauvignon blancs. While this wine is still fresh, bright and clean, it has more green herb aromas, and tastes lighter than most of its Marlborough counterparts. In many ways, this makes it more food friendly, especially with fresh seafood. It's good value and a lively style.

🛒 Specialist wine stores or www.waimeaestates.co.nz

2007 Spring Creek Marlborough Sauvignon Blanc

$19–20 ☆☆☆☆ Screwcap

This is one of the best sauvignon blancs in the book this year – fresh, ripe and full of gooseberry flavours and zing. It's an easy-to-love dry white wine.

🛒 Specialist wine stores or www.springcreekestate.co.nz

2007 Spy Valley Marlborough Sauvignon Blanc

$19–20 ☆☆☆☆ Screwcap

Great stuff, as always, this big-name sauvignon blanc is from New Zealand's largest wine region – Marlborough. In the space of about a decade, Spy Valley has grown from an unknown place to a high-quality wine brand; and with good reason. This sauvignon blanc is fresh, vibrant, zingy with good weight and length.

🛒 Widely available

2007 Staete Landt Marlborough Sauvignon Blanc

$22–23 ☆☆☆½ Screwcap

Modern Marlborough sauvignon blanc driven by big, sweet, tropical fruit flavours and a passionfruity, long finish. Serve lightly chilled on a summer's day.

🛒 Specialist wine stores or www.staetelandt.co.nz

2007 Stoneleigh Marlborough Rapaura Series Sauvignon Blanc

$22–23 ☆☆☆½ Screwcap

Full-bodied sauvignon blanc that is brimming over with tropical fruit flavours. Like sunshine in a glass.

🛒 Widely available

2007 Stoneleigh Marlborough Sauvignon Blanc

$17–18 ☆☆☆½ Screwcap

This is a fresh, dry, intense Marlborough sauvignon blanc – one of the longest-lived Kiwi wine brands in these days of ever-growing brands. Easily good value in taste and for money.

Widely available

2006 Stone Paddock Hawke's Bay Sauvignon Blanc

$18–20 ☆☆☆ Screwcap

Soft, simple, light Hawke's Bay sauvignon blanc. Average value at this price.

Specialist wine stores or www.paritua.com

2007 Taylors Adelaide Hills Sauvignon Blanc

$18–20 ☆☆☆☆ Screwcap

It may conjure up coals to Newcastle – Australian sauvignon blanc to New Zealand – but this wine breaks the mould with its cool, crisp Adelaide Hills reinterpretation of this grape variety. Buy it.

Widely available

2007 Te Awa Hawke's Bay Sauvignon Blanc

$20–22 ☆☆☆☆ Screwcap

When it comes to sauvignon blanc, Hawke's Bay is often forgotten, but wines like this deliciously full-bodied, rounded and intensely fruit-flavoured version provide great drinking.

Liquor stores or www.teawa.com

2007 Te Mania Sauvignon Blanc $18–19 ☆☆☆½ Screwcap

The small, Nelson-based, family-owned Te Mania winery produces this fresh, quintessentially Kiwi-tasting sauvignon blanc. Like most from Nelson, it has flavours of greengages (a green plum variety) and this wine has a lingering, zingy finish.

🛒 Specialist wine stores or www.temaniawines.co.nz

2007 Teviotdale Single Vineyard Sauvignon Blanc

$19–20 ☆☆☆☆ Screwcap

Like top chefs, top winemakers – such as Alan McCorkindale – get there via a well-honed understanding of what creates great flavour. This is a weighty, full-bodied, deliciously good Kiwi sauvignon blanc made by one of New Zealand's best winemakers. Look no further for great-tasting summer drinking.

🛒 Specialist wine stores

2007 The Crossings Marlborough Sauvignon Blanc

$19–20 ☆☆☆☆ Screwcap

Wow! Here's a refreshingly bright sauvignon blanc that is, thankfully, devoid of the over-the-top tropical tastes present in too many Kiwi whites today. By contrast, this wine is flinty, fresh and slightly sancerre-like (which is the biggest compliment you can pay to a good Kiwi sauvignon). Great value.

🛒 Widely available

2007 The Ned Sauvignon Blanc

$18–19 ☆☆☆½ Screwcap

Juicy, sweet, tropical fruit flavours give this wine huge appeal from the first sip. It is almost off-dry in style but nicely balanced for daytime drinking – try it lightly chilled in the afternoon at the beach, the park or at home just prior to a summer BBQ.

🛒 Widely available

2007 Thornbury Marlborough Sauvignon Blanc

$20–21 ☆☆☆ Screwcap

Zingy acids and green fruity aromas and flavours combine in this sauvignon blanc from New Zealand's biggest wine region.

Widely available

2007 Three Stones Marlborough Sauvignon Blanc

$19–20 ☆☆☆½ Screwcap

Tropical fruit in a glass – that's the best description of this off-dry Marlborough sauvignon blanc, which is made for everyday drinking. It's a light but clean and fresh style.

Widely available

2007 Timara Sauvignon Blanc $12–13 ☆☆☆ Screwcap

A very light but clean and fresh sauvignon blanc with hints of green herbs, kiwifruit and gooseberry in the aroma and a light, soft finish.

Widely available

2007 Tohu Marlborough Mugwi Sauvignon Blanc

$22–24 ☆☆☆ Screwcap

A very different style to the main Tohu sauvignon blanc (below). This wine has a defined green kiwifruit edge to its flavour spectrum. Drink with fresh fish.

Specialist wine stores or www.tohuwines.co.nz

2007 Tohu Marlborough Sauvignon Blanc

$19–20 ☆☆☆☆ Screwcap

It's too easy to love this white wine. Fresh, clean and zingy? Yes. Intense, balanced and full of flavour? Definitely – and that's what gives it an edge.

Specialist wine stores or www.tohuwines.co.nz

2007 Trinity Hill Hawke's Bay Sauvignon Blanc
$19–20 ☆☆☆☆ Screwcap

Like so many good Hawke's Bay sauvignon blancs, this is a soft, tropical-fruit-scented delight. Its rounded, fleshy body and lingering, clean flavours make it a really good summer, autumn, winter or anytime white wine. Good value too.

🛒 Widely available or www.trinityhill.com

2007 Tupari Sauvignon Blanc $16–18 ☆☆☆ Screwcap

Grapefruits and lemons seem to leap out of each mouthful of this intense, zingy Marlborough sauvignon blanc. Chill and enjoy during the daytime.

🛒 Online at www.tupariwines.com

2007 Twin Islands Marlborough Sauvignon Blanc
$18–19 ☆☆☆½ Screwcap

With its subtle and well-styled rebranding, its consistently good price-to-flavour ratio and its varietal purity, this is a great-value sauvignon blanc. Intense on the front palate, soft in the middle and easy all the way. Good buying.

🛒 Widely available

2007 Vavasour Awatere Valley Sauvignon Blanc
$19–20 ☆☆☆☆ Screwcap

The 2006 version of this savvy was one of the star wines in the book, and this 2007 version is another outstandingly good drink. Fresher, more vibrant and with pure, focused, steely, appley, gooseberry flavours . . . none of which really does justice to this southern Marlborough sauvignon blanc. Too easy to love.

🛒 Widely available or www.vavasour.com

2007 Vidal Marlborough Sauvignon Blanc

$18–19 ☆☆☆½ Screwcap

This bright, fresh, youthful sauvignon blanc offers great value, deliciously zingy flavours and a long finish in every mouthful. Good value for a high-class sauvignon blanc.

Widely available

2007 Villa Maria Cellar Selection Marlborough Sauvignon Blanc

$22–23 ☆☆☆☆ Screwcap

Top marks to Villa Maria for its superlative sauvignon blanc under $25 – and with change left over. This stunningly intense, vibrant, passionfruity and still somehow restrained sauvignon blanc is great drinking and delivers on every cent you pay for it.

Widely available

2007 Villa Maria Marlborough Sauvignon Blanc

$17–18 ☆☆☆½ Screwcap

This is New Zealand sauvignon blanc at its best because of its sheer value for money and distinctiveness. I love the gooseberry freshness and hints of tropical fruit in this wine.

Widely available

2007 Waimea Bolitho Sauvignon Blanc $21–22 ☆☆☆☆ Screwcap

As the top wine of the vast Waimea Estates range, this is a medium-bodied sauvignon blanc. It's full of upfront fruity flavours of fresh kiwifruit, green herbs and has a lingering finish.

Specialist wine stores or www.waimeaestates.co.nz

2007 Waimea Nelson Sauvignon Blanc $21–22 ☆☆☆☆ Screwcap

This is a beautiful, bright, fresh Nelson sauvignon blanc, and like most whites from this region it is a taste departure from Marlborough's usual sauvignons. Lighter, more food-friendly in flavour with a delicious, fresh herb edge to it, this tastes fab with fresh fish.

🛒 Specialist wine stores or www.waimeaestates.co.nz

2007 Waipara Hills Marlborough Sauvignon Blanc
$18–19 ☆☆☆½ Screwcap

Fresh, bright South Island sauvignon blanc – vibrant, clean and great value.

🛒 Specialist wine stores

2007 Wairau River Sauvignon Blanc $20 ☆☆☆☆ Screwcap

Wow! This lovely sauvignon blanc is not just soft, fresh and bright, but it's drier than most, making it food friendly, particularly with fresh oysters – the best you can get!

🛒 Widely available or www.wairauriverwines.co.nz

2007 Walnut Block Marlborough Sauvignon Blanc
$23–24 ☆☆☆☆ Screwcap

Walnut Block is a brand-new wine label from Marlborough – and this is a top-tasting sauvignon blanc. Intense, vibrant, zingy and great value.

🛒 Liquor stores and specialist wine stores

2007 Wild South Marlborough Sauvignon Blanc
$19–20 ☆☆☆½ Screwcap

Vibrant, intense Marlborough sauvignon blanc with fresh herb flavours, lively acids and a soft, smooth finish.

🛒 Specialist wine stores or www.wildsouthwines.co.nz

2007 William Thomas Marlborough Sauvignon Blanc
$24–25 ☆☆☆ Screwcap

From a small, relatively new Marlborough winery comes this clean, fresh, well-made sauvignon blanc with its zingy kiwifruit and gooseberry flavours. Good summertime drinking, served lightly chilled.

🛒 Specialist wine stores

2007 Woollaston Sauvignon Blanc $19–20 ☆☆☆½ Screwcap

This is a fresh and very tropical-tasting sauvignon blanc from one of the bigger Nelson wineries, Woollaston Estate – a great place to visit to enjoy the underground cellar door, as well as the wines.

🛒 Specialist wine stores or www.woollaston.co.nz

Semillon

'Sem-ee-yon'

For some, semillon will never be great, but it is an essential ingredient in many of the world's greatest dessert wines (including, perhaps most famously, sauternes from Bordeaux). It is also responsible for one of the world's unique wines – dry semillon, early harvested, from Australia's Hunter Valley. The best Hunter Valley semillons can last for decades in the bottle, evolving into a white that tastes like an old, bone-dry chardonnay – but I digress. These wines here are light, refreshing, and often blended with other grapes to add body. They are simple, everyday whites, although a couple are far better than that, as their presence here attests.

Star semillon

2006 Jacob's Creek Semillon Chardonnay

$10–12 ☆☆☆ Screwcap

This wine is a simple, light white with lots of innate citrusy freshness from the chardonnay, which teams up well with the slightly herby zing of the semillon.

🛒 Widely available

2006 Nottage Hill Semillon Sauvignon Blanc

$10–12 ☆☆☆ Screwcap

Light, fresh, simple white wine from Australia. Chill it and enjoy cool at the beach in summer.

🛒 Widely available

Soave

'Swav-ey'

2006 Bolla Soave $18–19 ☆☆☆

This is a simple, soft Italian white with slightly nutty flavours. A good wine to drink during the daytime or late afternoon, especially in summer, with light, salty nibbles.

🛒 Glengarry stores in the North Island and specialist wine stores nationwide

Star soave

2006 Pasqua Soave Classico

$15–16 ☆☆☆½

A light, simple Italian white with nutty aromas and flavours, making it a good with-nibbles white.

🛒 Glengarry stores in the North Island and specialist wine stores nationwide

Verdelho

'Ver-dello'

2007 Esk Valley Verdelho $20–21 ☆☆☆ Screwcap

Light in taste, though not in alcohol, this alternative white wine is made from the verdelho grape, a rarity in New Zealand. A good, refreshing wine for summertime drinking – serve lightly chilled.

Widely available

2007 Sandalford Margaret River Verdelho

$18–20 ☆☆☆½ Screwcap

Western Australian verdelho with light, floral aromas and a dry finish. Chill very lightly and enjoy year round with toasted, salted almonds.

Liquor stores and specialist wine stores

Verdicchio

'Ver-deek-ee-oh'

Verdicchio is an Italian white grape from Central Italy, capable of producing top-quality, fresh, everyday whites, such as the one in this chapter.

Garofoli Verdicchio Anfora $17–18 ☆☆☆☆☆

Looking for a fresh, dry white wine that tastes near-perfect with seafood? Try this lovely, light, slightly salty Italian white. It's fantastically refreshing, served lightly chilled. Good value.

Sovrano, Auckland, phone (09) 271 5969

Vernaccia

'Ver-nach-ea'

2006 Vernaccia de San Gimignano $16–17 ☆☆☆½

Looking for a wine for lunch today? Try this aromatic fresh and bright Tuscan white wine, which is uniquely savoury, dry and cleansing in taste and style.

🛒 Wine stores or for stockists contact Prodotti d'Italia, phone (09) 276 7140 or www.pdi.co.nz

Viognier

'Vee-oh-nee-ay'

Kiwi winemakers everywhere – from Auckland, Gisborne, Hawke's Bay, the Wairarapa and Nelson – are vaunting viognier as The Next Big White Wine Thing. It will probably never actually make it to the big time, but viognier is increasingly popular.

Traditionally, viognier – a Rhône Valley grape variety – has been difficult to grow due to it being sensitive to both wind and cold. Its most famous expression is in French Condrieu, but even there this grape variety all but died out, in part because of how difficult viognier is to grow in the vineyard. However, there is an increasing amount of viognier in the New Zealand national vineyard, mostly in the North Island and particularly in Gisborne. It has potential for making small amounts of high-quality, rounded, dry whites. Watch this space.

Star viognier

2007 Villa Maria Cellar Selection Hawke's Bay Viognier

$24–25 ☆☆☆☆

2007 Anchorage Hawke's Bay Viognier $19–20 ☆☆☆ Screwcap

For all those tiring of wines made from mainstream grape varieties, here's a slight style departure – a viognier from Hawke's Bay. Medium bodied, peachy and nearly bone dry, it is a good daytime or late-afternoon wine.

Specialist wine stores or www.anchoragewines.co.nz

2006 Commissioner's Block Viognier $16–17 ☆☆☆ Screwcap

Just as long as you expect this wine to taste slightly sweet, you'll cope with its intense peachy flavours and verging-on-medium-sweet style. Best to serve lightly chilled with salted cashews.

Widely available or www.neqtarwines.com.au

2006 Huntaway Gisborne Viognier $19–20 ☆☆☆ Screwcap

Spicy, peachy and light – lovely summertime white from Gisborne.

Widely available

2007 Mission Reserve Viognier $24–25 ☆☆☆

If it ever seemed as if viognier was The Next Big Thing, put all such thoughts aside. It's a tricky grape to grow, sensitive to wind and often not a high-cropping variety. That said, the results of tenacious viticulture can be wines like this one – soft, smooth and peachy. An interesting, alternative white wine.

Liquor stores and specialist wine stores

2007 Moana Park Gimblett Road Viognier
$19–20 ☆☆☆ Screwcap

A peachy-tasting viognier with medium body, hints of spice and stonefruit flavours.

Specialist wine stores or www.moanapark.co.nz

2007 Ti Point Viognier $19–20 ☆☆☆½ Screwcap

Winemaker Tracy Haslam has made a fresh, light, aromatic white wine here with grapes grown in Hawke's Bay. Its flavours verge on pears and peaches and it is just off-dry and medium bodied. Good daytime or late-afternoon summer drinking.

Glengarry stores and other specialist wine stores or www.tipoint.co.nz

2006 Trinity Hill Gimblett Gravels Viognier

$19–20 ☆☆☆ Screwcap

Light Hawke's Bay viognier with soft, fleshy peachy flavours and an off-dry finish. Nice summertime wine.

🛒 Specialist wine stores or www.trinityhill.com

2007 Vidal East Coast Viognier $19–20 ☆☆☆½ Screwcap

Viognier is fresh in our mouths and our minds right now, mostly because there is barely any of it around. The highly sensitive viognier grape dislikes wind and some cool conditions, but when it does behave itself this is one of the roundest, peachiest white wines around – with the added bonus of being dry. This one is a great introduction to the style.

🛒 Widely available

Star viognier

2007 Villa Maria Cellar Selection Hawke's Bay Viognier

$24–25 ☆☆☆☆ Screwcap

If you're looking for The Next Big Thing, viognier might just be it – for those tiring of the ever-present pinot gris, that is. And this viognier is one of the best Kiwi versions I've yet tried. Ripe and peachy in taste, it is full bodied and lingering on the finish. A good late-afternoon wine.

🛒 Specialist wine stores or www.villamaria.co.nz

2007 Waimea Nelson Viognier $17–19 ☆☆☆ Screwcap

Light, floral and fresh in taste, this off-dry aromatic white is an interesting alternative to your usual faves to kick off the night.

🛒 Specialist wine stores or www.waimeaestates.co.nz

2006 Zilzie Viognier $18–19 ☆☆☆½ Screwcap

Viognier is one of the most popular alternative white grapes in Australia these days and this is one of the best versions around – spicy, off-dry (which adds flavour appeal) and good value too.

🛒 Specialist wine stores

Rosés

Rosé rocks. Ever since the world's most famous pink-coloured wine, Mateus, relaunched its 'Drink Pink' campaign earlier this millennium, blush, rosé and pink wines have been summer's hottest wine everywhere from Europe and the UK to the USA, Australia and New Zealand.

Rosé can be made from virtually any red grape variety, though some are obviously better suited than others to what is basically a more dilute version of themselves. Most pink wines come at a relatively low cost, so this chapter offers a good insight into where the rosé scene is at in New Zealand right now.

Star rosé

2006 Clayridge Marlborough Pinot Rosé

$22–23 ☆☆☆☆

2006 Armantes Old Bush Vine Rosé $16–17 ☆☆☆½

Few rosés are as robust in flavour, fruitiness and body as this big gutsy Spanish garnacha (aka grenache). Full bodied in the shape of a red wine, but crisp and refreshing like a white, providing it's served lightly chilled.

Specialist wine stores or contact Bennett & Deller for stockists near you, phone (09) 378 9463

2007 Askerne Rosé $16–17 ☆☆☆ Screwcap

This Hawke's Bay rosé is definitely off-dry in style with sweet strawberry and raspberry flavours, and a medium body. Serve lightly chilled.

🛒 Specialist wine stores or www.askerne.co.nz

2007 Ata Rangi Summer Rosé $20–22 ☆☆☆☆ Screwcap

It's no surprise to find a great rosé from the small, quality-focused Ata Rangi winery in Martinborough. This is luscious, off-dry but well balanced – chill it and love it in summer or after work around the fire in winter; yes, you'll be surprised how versatile good rosé is.

🛒 Specialist wine stores, wine bars and www.atarangi.co.nz

Star rosé

2006 Clayridge Marlborough Pinot Rosé

$22–23 ☆☆☆☆ Screwcap

Marlborough winemaker Mike Just is one of this country's dabbest hands at aromatic white wines, and this soft, light rosé made from pinot noir is also good. Firm acids underpin fresh berryfruit flavours. Serve lightly chilled.

🛒 Specialist wine stores or www.clayridge.net.nz

2007 Clearview Estate Black Reef Blush $23–24 ☆☆☆☆ Screwcap

Deep ruby in colour and vibrantly fruity in style, this is a great Kiwi rosé. Love its firm acids, long finish and deliciously fruity upfront style.

🛒 Specialist wine stores or www.clearviewestate.co.nz

2007 Crawford Farm Rosé $20–22 ☆☆☆☆ Screwcap

More of a light red than just a rosé, this is a lovely off-dry wine made with grapes grown in several of New Zealand's main wine regions. Serve lightly chilled – perfect at the beach or round your favourite pool in summer.

Widely available

2007 Forrest Estate Marlborough Rosé
$19–20 ☆☆☆½ Screwcap

Always a good-value, though slightly off-dry rosé. This wine is deeper in colour than many blush-pink wines and it's also slightly weightier. Be sure to serve lightly chilled to tone down the off-dry style.

Specialist wine stores or www.forrestwines.co.nz

2006 Kew Wild Rosé $15–16 ☆☆☆ Screwcap

This is the most popular wine from the small Kew Winery in Gisborne. Made with the partial use of wild yeasts, hence the name, this is an interesting, fresh, light red and should be served lightly chilled.

Specialist wine stores or email info@kew.co.nz

2007 Kim Crawford Pansy! Rosé
$19–20 ☆☆☆☆ Screwcap

It's not only the bright pink packaging that gives this wine its instant appeal. This light-red rosé is made from merlot grapes grown in Gisborne, so it has fresh berry flavours coupled with firm acids, the latter adding zing and balance.

Widely available

2007 La Mura Rosé Sicilia $14–16 ☆☆☆½ Screwcap

Made from the red nero d'avola grape, this soft, fresh, strawberry-tasting Italian red wine offers fresh, luscious, off-dry summer drinking. Serve very lightly chilled and definitely with food.

Specialist wine stores or for stockists contact Prodotti d'Italia, phone (09) 276 7140 or www.pdi.co.nz

2007 Matua Valley North Island Rosé $14–16 ☆☆☆ Screwcap

Light, fresh, simple rosé with robust body, but noticeably off-dry so make sure you chill it before taking it to the beach or even just the back garden.

Widely available

2004 Moana Park Pascoe Series Rosé $19–20 ☆☆☆ Screwcap

This is a simple rosé that's very light and off-dry with sweet berry flavours. Chill and drink now; it's already four years old and shouldn't be held on to any longer than this.

Specialist wine stores or www.moanapark.co.nz

Monkey Bay Rosé $10–12 ☆☆☆ Screwcap

This lively, pink non-vintage wine has sweet fruity flavours and an off-dry finish to add appeal. Chill lightly to enjoy at its best.

Widely available

2007 Morton Estate Musetta Rosé $19–20 ☆☆☆☆ Screwcap

The appealing red hue of 'musetta' rosé is due to the blend of merlot and malbec (an intensely coloured red grape). It's just off-dry in style but has lots of vibrant freshness in taste, impressive body and lingering length of flavour. Great value for money.

Widely available

2007 Mystery Creek Waikato Syrah Rosé $16–17 ☆☆☆ Screwcap

This light, fresh, deeply coloured pink wine is made from the syrah grape. Bright and clean in style, it's a refreshing wine to drink year round, with more body than many pink wines and a near-dry finish. Chill lightly.

Specialist wine stores or www.mysterycreekwines.com

2007 Richmond Plains Nelson Monarch Road Rosé
$19–20 ☆☆☆ Screwcap

This small Nelson winery makes a large range of wines, from this fresh, strawberry fresh-tasting rosé through to light whites and soft reds. This is off-dry, so serve lightly chilled.

Specialist wine stores

2007 Sandalford Protégé Rosé $19–20 ☆☆☆ Screwcap

This is a light, simple rosé with bright, off-dry sweet fruit flavours. Simple, everyday number for the beach.

Widely available

2007 Selaks Premium Selection Merlot Rosé
$14–15 ☆☆☆½ Screwcap

Merlot's soft, sweet berry flavours make this wine hugely appealing – and it's off-dry to entice drinkers even more. Be sure to chill lightly to enjoy at its best, and serve with pistachios.

Widely available

2007 Sileni Cellar Selection Cellar Selection Rosé
$19–20 ☆☆☆☆ Screwcap

Winemaker Grant Edmonds is a master of rosé, and here he has crafted a fresh, strawberry-tasting dark-pink wine from Hawke's Bay. Love the intense acids and lingering finish here.

Specialist wine stores or www.sileni.co.nz

2006 Stoneleigh Marlborough Pinot Noir Rosé
$16–17 ☆☆☆½ Screwcap

This is soft, strawberry-like in flavour and definitely off-dry. Chill it and drink as a lunchtime wine.

Widely available

2006 Taylors Promised Land White Cabernet Rosé
$14–15 ☆☆☆ Screwcap

Deep pink in colour, berry-like in flavour and off-dry in style – a good summer drink, serve lightly chilled.

Widely available

2007 Te Mania Nelson Pinot Noir Rosé $19–20 ☆☆☆ Screwcap

Pinot noir makes soft, strawberry-tasting pink wines, such as this Nelson version. It's off-dry with attractive berryfruit flavours. Serve lightly chilled to enjoy at its best.

Specialist wine stores

2007 Trinity Hill Hawke's Bay Rosé $18–19 ☆☆☆½ Screwcap

Good pink wine is easy to find these days, but the best ones still tower head and shoulders over the rest. This is one of them. I like its weighty body, fresh strawberry flavours and dry finish.

Widely available

2007 Triplebank Marlborough Pinot Noir Rosé
$18–20 ☆☆☆½ Screwcap

Deep pink in colour, with bright, fresh strawberry flavours and an off-dry style, this is good value for summertime drinking especially. That said, its medium-bodied style and weight give it the versatility to drink and enjoy mid-winter, lightly chilled, early in the evening.

Widely available

2007 Twin Totara Rosé $18–19 ☆☆☆ Screwcap

West Auckland winemaker Shayne Cox turns out this soft, light pink wine for the evocative Twin Totara brand. It's fresh, clean and great drinking at lunchtime or serve it lightly chilled with spicy food.

Cellar Select wine stores or contact Twin Totara Wines, email montyhaddon@clear.net.nz

2007 Unison Hawke's Bay Rosé $19–20 ☆☆☆☆ Screwcap

This flavoursome Hawke's Bay dark-pink wine is one of New Zealand's best rosés each year – delicious with and without summer food. Ideal lightly cooled on a hot day.

Specialist wine stores or www.unisonvineyard.co.nz

2007 Vavasour Awatere Valley Rosé $17–19 ☆☆☆½ Screwcap

This bright crimson rosé is definitely made in an off-dry style, but is a beautiful balance between berryfruit flavours and fresh acidity. It's a great food wine in summertime – serve lightly chilled.

Liquor stores and some supermarkets or www.vavasour.com

2007 Villa Maria Hawke's Bay Rosé $17–18 ☆☆☆ Screwcap

Soft, simple Hawke's Bay rosé with zingy acids adding a pleasant tang to this refreshing everyday wine. Serve lightly chilled.

Widely available

2007 Woollaston Pinot Noir Rosé $19–20 ☆☆☆ Screwcap

Light-pink Nelson rosé made from pinot noir grapes for everyday drinking and especially good with seafood at lunch on the weekend. Serve lightly chilled.

Specialist wine stores or www.woollaston.co.nz

Red wines

Beaujolais

'Bo-jol-lay'

Beaujolais can range from light and insubstantial (like beaujolais nouveau) through to weighty, serious Villages wines. Few of the best make it to New Zealand, but those that do tend to sit in the middle somewhere, especially in this price range. These wines are exactly the sort of reds to serve lightly chilled with a toasted ham or prosciutto sandwich and the best cheese you can afford to melt all over it – with a dollop of creamy mustard on the side.

2007 Georges Duboeuf Beaujolais-Villages $17–18 ☆☆☆

Beaujolais can be one of the softest, fruitiest, lightest red wines in the world, and this little everyday version is all of those things. Its flavours are of berries and light spice.

🛒 Glengarry stores in the North Island and specialist wine stores nationwide

Cabernet sauvignon, cabernet franc and blends

'Cab-err-nay so-vin-yon'

If you had to come up with one word to describe cabernet sauvignon it would have to be 'serious'. More than any other red wine, cabernet sauvignon is a heady style of red designed – as many winemakers are particularly fond of saying – for those who like to operate in life from the neck up. Cabernet sauvignon's spiritual home is in Bordeaux, France, but it is grown almost everywhere that wine is made and is most revered for its famously good top-shelf reds from California, Chile, Western Australia and Coonawarra in South Australia.

In this price range Australia has the category cornered, although there is a small but growing number of very good wines made from cabernet sauvignon under $20 from New Zealand. This is a difficult area for New Zealand to compete in, however, since this country does not have the sheer economy of scale nor the climate to produce loads of affordable cabernet sauvignons.

Star cabernet

2005 Sandalford Protégé Cabernet Merlot Margaret River

$20–21 ☆☆☆☆

2006 Angus The Bull Cabernet Sauvignon

$20–22 ☆☆☆☆ Screwcap

A quick glance at this label seems to say: 'buy a great steak right now' – and the first whiff and sip back this up. This is a big, gutsy Australian cabernet sauvignon, full of body, firm fruit flavours and a long, fresh finish.

🛒 Liquor stores and specialist wine stores

2001 Augustus Cabernet Sauvignon Merlot $19–20 ☆☆☆

Interesting oldish Spanish red made from the traditional French grapes, cabernet sauvignon and merlot. This wine is earthy and slightly rustic in style and good with slow-cooked meat as a hearty winter red.

🛒 Sabato, Mt Eden, Auckland, phone (09) 630 8751
or www.sabato.co.nz

2004 Baritone Maxim 1000 Cabernet Shiraz $16–17 ☆☆☆½

Its one-litre capacity makes this big bottle also a big bargain, in terms of sheer good value for size and dollars spent. It is soft and rounded, ready to drink now rather than waiting any longer – and this wine is made as a daily quaffer rather than anything to keep hanging on to.

🛒 New World and Pak'nSave supermarkets

2005 Brown Brothers Cabernet Sauvignon

$18–19 ☆☆☆½ Screwcap

An oldie but a goodie, especially now it's sealed with a screwcap. This lovely big red is packed with classic blackcurrant and blackberry flavours and firm tannins, making it a rewarding everyday red that is good value for money.

🛒 Widely available

2006 Clearview Estate Cape Kidnappers Cabernet Merlot

$22–24 ☆☆☆½ Screwcap

To describe this wine as clean, fresh and bright only begins to capture the style of it, but it's also a serious step up from Kiwi reds of old – especially good at this price.

Specialist wine stores or www.clearviewestate.co.nz

2005 Climbing Cabernet Sauvignon $20–21 ☆☆☆☆ Screwcap

What a bargain. Big blackcurrant and blackberry flavours combine in a full-bodied but surprisingly elegant red wine – the surprise is that it costs so little and delivers so much. Love this one.

Specialist wine stores

2005 Cockatoo Ridge Cabernet Merlot $12–13 ☆☆☆½ Screwcap

At three years old, this Aussie blend of cabernet sauvignon with merlot is slightly older than many reds we drink in this country; it's all the better for it too – still clean and fresh with lots of soft berry flavours and a lingering finish.

Widely available

2005 Commissioner's Block Cabernet Sauvignon

$15–16 ☆☆☆½ Screwcap

A lively and instantly recognisable Australian cabernet sauvignon with pronounced capsicum aromas and flavours – and a lingering spicy finish.

Widely available or www.robertsestatewines.com.au

2005 Cookoothama Cabernet Merlot $20–21 ☆☆☆½ Screwcap

Here's another Australian blend of cabernet sauvignon with merlot that offers very good value. Rich, ripe black fruit flavours are supported by sturdy oak and a full-bodied style.

Glengarry stores in the North Island and specialist wine stores nationwide

2005 Deen De Bortoli Vat 9 Cabernet Sauvignon

$15–16 ☆☆☆½ Screwcap

A hearty big Australian red with fresh minty flavours. Enjoy this wine with tasty sausages or roast beef.

🛒 Glengarry stores in the North Island and other specialist wine stores

2006 Grant Burge Barossa Cabernet Sauvignon Merlot

$19–20 ☆☆☆½ Screwcap

A blend of cabernet sauvignon and merlot from top shiraz producer, Grant Burge winery in the Barossa Valley, that offers good value for money. Hints of capsicum and blackberry are the flavours here.

🛒 Liquor stores and specialist wine stores

2006 Hardys Nottage Hill Cabernet Sauvignon $10–12 ☆☆☆

Another simple everyday Australian red offering good value for a party or as an easy BBQ wine.

🛒 Widely available

2006 Hardys Nottage Hill Cabernet Shiraz $10–12 ☆☆☆

It's a good-value red, this Australian blend of cabernet sauvignon and shiraz, with simple, soft fruit flavours. Hints of spice and a medium body.

🛒 Widely available

2006 Hardys Oomoo Cabernet Sauvignon $17-18 ☆☆☆½

Well known, well liked and with good reason. This good-value Australian cabernet sauvignon is priced to appeal, offering lots of ripe current and fruit flavours.

🛒 Widely available

2006 Jacob's Creek Cabernet Sauvignon

$13–14 ☆☆☆ Screwcap

This is a big red, even in terms of alcohol – 14 per cent – which is no mean feat in a wine intended for everyday drinking. Be sure to pour yourself a smaller amount than usual to compensate for this. It's simple and fruity in flavour, with classic cabernet sauvignon's blackcurrant aromas and tastes.

🛒 Widely available

2005 Jacob's Creek Reserve Cabernet Sauvignon

$18–20 ☆☆☆☆ Screwcap

This is great value for money, for a bold, full-bodied Australian cabernet sauvignon. It will soften and improve in the bottle, if you're willing to buy a few bottles and age them somewhere cool and dark. Otherwise, enjoy it at a dinner party.

🛒 Widely available

2005 Knappstein Clare Valley Cabernet Merlot

$23–24 ☆☆☆½ Screwcap

Australia's Clare Valley is far better known for shiraz than for cabernet and merlot, but this is a firm, fresh and very good Aussie blend of the latter. Outstanding everyday drinking.

🛒 Liquor stores and specialist wine stores

2005 Leasingham Clare Valley Magnus Cabernet Merlot

$22–23 ☆☆☆½ Screwcap

Like so many Australian reds, the flavour of this one is characterised by rich toasty oak, a hint of mint and loads of blackberry. It's so big, even at four years old, that this wine definitely demands a large, juicy steak to go with it.

🛒 Widely available

2007 Mission Hawke's Bay Cabernet Sauvignon

$16–18 ☆☆☆½ Screwcap

Big-name Hawke's Bay winery, the Mission Estate, in Taradale, Napier, makes a vast number of reliably good everyday wines, including this lovely, vibrant and fresh red cabernet sauvignon. Very modern, and great value.

🛒 Widely available

2006 Montes Cabernet Sauvignon Carmenere $22–23 ☆☆☆½

This is a big-bodied, full-flavoured, intensely coloured Chilean red. It's a style departure from most cabernet sauvignons since it is blended with carmenere – a French grape that is now best known in Chile. If you like big reds, you'll love this.

🛒 Glengarry stores in the North Island and specialist wine stores nationwide

2006 Montes Classic Cabernet Sauvignon $19–20 ☆☆☆☆

Chile is home to some exciting red wines, which taste good and provide surprisingly great value for money. This is one of the best currently available in New Zealand. Full bodied, packed with ripe blackcurrant flavours supported by spicy oak, and a long finish. Very good value.

🛒 Glengarry stores in the North Island and specialist wine stores nationwide

2006 Piccini Cabernet Merlot $15–16 ☆☆☆½

Instantly lovable Sicilian red blend of cabernet sauvignon and merlot. Lovely and ripe with rich blackcurrant flavours and hints of savoury notes.

🛒 Supermarkets, wine stores or for stockists contact Prodotti d'Italia, phone (09) 276 7140 or www.pdi.co.nz

2006 Piccini Cabernet Syrah $15–16 ☆☆☆☆

Sicily's warm climate shines through in this super-value red wine; a new-wave style from the south of Italy.

🛒 Supermarkets, wine stores or for stockists contact Prodotti d'Italia, phone (09) 276 7140 or www.pdi.co.nz

2004 Pirrimimma McLaren Vale Cabernet Sauvignon $24–25 ☆☆☆½

This is a lovely everyday red from McLaren Vale, south of Adelaide. Rich, sweet, berry aromas intermingle with spicy oak flavours.

🛒 Specialist wine stores

2004 Plantagenet Great Southern Cabernet Sauvignon $19–20 ☆☆☆☆

It's not only the label that's restrained in this Australian cabernet sauvignon. This wine offers great value for money and lots of variation on the usual cabernet theme – it's big, yes, but also elegant. Try it.

🛒 Widely available

2004 Plantagenet Omrah Cabernet Sauvignon $16–18 ☆☆☆☆

Always great value, this wine offers lots of elegance, surprising complexity and layers of flavour at this price. It's four years old now and still tastes good – drink with a venison steak on the BBQ.

🛒 Widely available

2006 Preece Cabernet Sauvignon $18–20 ☆☆☆½ Screwcap

An instantly recognisable Australian cabernet sauvignon with pronounced capsicum flavours intermingling with berryfruit tastes. Good for everyday drinking, nothing more.

🛒 Liquor stores and specialist wine stores

2005 Rolling Cabernet Merlot $18–19 ☆☆☆½ Screwcap

If the evocative painterly label of this wine doesn't woo you, its soft berry flavours will. This is a clean and fresh, everyday drinking Australian blend of cabernet sauvignon with merlot grapes – smooth, velvety and slightly smoky in taste.

Specialist wine stores

2006 Saints Hawke's Bay Cabernet Merlot
$16–18 ☆☆☆½ Screwcap

If you're a die-hard fan of New Zealand cabernet sauvignon, then this wine is one of the best-value versions of it on the market today. Packed with sweet blackberry and raspberry flavours, its backbone of oak adds body and flavour interest.

Widely available

Star cabernet

2005 Sandalford Protégé Cabernet Merlot Margaret River

$20–21 ☆☆☆☆ Screwcap

Talk about stunning value – which is no surprise, given the top cabernet sauvignons that this Western Australian winery makes. Here is a fresh, fruity but multilayered red wine, which takes you by surprise considering the $20 you'll pay for its complex flavours. Love the spicy berry flavours and the lingering finish.

Specialist wine stores or contact Burleigh Trading for stockists near you, phone (09) 480 0789

2005 Stone Paddock Cabernet Sauvignon $18–20 ☆☆☆ Screwcap

Fresh, fruit-driven, elegant Hawke's Bay cabernet sauvignon – and very good value.

Specialist wine stores

2005 Taltarni 3 Monks Cabernet Merlot $24–25 ☆☆☆☆

There are so many Australian red wines today that it's tricky trying to pick the best from the rest, but this is easily a stand-out red. Blended from cabernet sauvignon and merlot, it's bright, fresh and has underlying weight, and robust body and flavours too.

🛒 Glengarry stores in the North Island and specialist wine stores nationwide

2004 Tapestry McLaren Vale Cabernet Merlot

$23–24 ☆☆☆½ Screwcap

It's four years old now, and definitely tasting like an aged wine, meaning it has developed past just primary fruit flavours into a mature cabernet with tastes of spice and soft oak coming through. Drink with slow-cooked beef in winter.

🛒 Widely available or www.tapestrywines.com.au

2004 Tatachilla Partners Cabernet Shiraz

$22–24 ☆☆☆½ Screwcap

This is a lively, young Australian blend of cabernet with shiraz – fresh, bright in flavours and needing a little time to soften out (or decant it for a couple of hours prior to serving). You don't need a posh glass wine decanter – a jug will do just fine. The point is to make the wine taste better, and air is a great friend to young wines.

🛒 Widely available

2005 Taylors Clare Valley Cabernet Sauvignon

$18–19 ☆☆☆½ Screwcap

Wines of this price can go one of two ways, but this is a great-value – and great-tasting – drop from the Clare Valley in Barossa, Australia. Ripe, sweet blackberries all the way from start to finish. A good everyday drop.

🛒 Widely available

2005 Taylors Eighty Acres Cabernet Shiraz Merlot

$19–20 ☆☆☆½ Screwcap

One of a trio of new wines under the Eighty Acres brand, this is my pick of the range. It's the driest in taste, with its blackberry-cabernet sauvignon flavours dominant in the blend. Shiraz adds sweet fruit appeal to this better-than-everyday red wine.

🛒 Widely available

2006 Taylors Promised Land Cabernet Merlot

$16–18 ☆☆☆½ Screwcap

It's nothing short of incredible the great value for money that Australia's low-priced reds offer. This blend of cabernet sauvignon and merlot is packed with flavour – ripe, intense blackberries to the fore with firm, fresh acids keeping it in check. Great value for money.

🛒 Widely available

2005 Trapiche Oak Cask Cabernet Sauvignon $15–16 ☆☆☆½

This is a good everyday Argentinian cabernet sauvignon that tastes best with a big juicy steak or rare roast beef, which matches its savoury and slightly rustic flavours.

🛒 Pak'nSave Wellington

2006 Twin Totara Cabernet Franc Merlot

$18–19 ☆☆☆½ Screwcap

West Auckland winemaker Shayne Cox turns out this soft Kiwi red blend of cabernet franc and merlot for the Twin Totara brand. It's an intense, surprisingly deeply flavoured red – no doubt due to the richness of the cabernet franc grape in this blend. Good value.

🛒 Cellar Select stores or contact Twin Totara Wines, email montyhaddon@clear.net.nz

2006 Vidal Hawke's Bay Merlot Cabernet Sauvignon

$19–20 ☆☆☆½ Screwcap

Here's a big, grippy red wine with lots of oomph, power and fruit-forward flavours. Think of a midwinter, round-the-fire type of wine and you have it in one. This is a good everyday drink.

Widely available

2006 Villa Maria Hawke's Bay Private Bin Merlot Cabernet Sauvignon

$17–18 ☆☆☆½ Screwcap

Good New Zealand red blend of merlot and cabernet sauvignon, both grown in Hawke's Bay. This is a step up from many Kiwi reds at this price, and good value for week-night drinking.

Widely available

2004 Wyndham Estate Bin 888 Cabernet Merlot

$14–15 ☆☆☆ Screwcap

Best known as an everyday red wine, this Australian blend of cabernet sauvignon with merlot is soft, light and fresh – better now it's under screwcap than it's ever been in the past. Good drinking for an after-work glass, before moving on to something more serious.

Widely available

2005 Zilzie Cabernet Sauvignon

$18–19 ☆☆☆½

It's unusual these days to spot an Australian cabernet sauvignon at this price without a screwcap.

Specialist wine stores

Carmenere

'Car-men-yehr'

Carmenere (or more properly, carménère) polarises wine drinkers. For some, it is never going to be one of the great stand-alone reds of the wine world, but it was, until last decade, one of the most mysterious grapes in the world.

For others, carmenere is relatively unknown. A meaty-tasting red grape, it found its way to Chile prior to the scourge of the vine-devastating louse, phylloxera, which wiped out masses of vineyards in Europe in the 1800s. When the vines were being built up again in Europe, post-phylloxera, carmenere never found its way back into the Bordeaux fold – hence its reputation as 'the forgotten grape of Bordeaux'.

Some would say with good reason too – this is not one of the great grapes of the world, hence its inclusion historically in Bordeaux reds as a blending component rather than a stand-alone varietal wine. The exception to this is in Chile, where carmenere and merlot have often been confused in the vineyard. Now it is acknowledged that many vines the Chileans once thought to be merlot are actually carmenere.

2004 Punta Nogal Carmenere $14–15 ☆☆☆½

This Chilean carmenere is made from grapes grown in the Colchagua Valley. It's an intensely fruit-driven red, and needs food to soften its staunch acids. Good everyday red for a BBQ.

🛒 Moore Wilson and selected supermarkets or contact Delmaine Fine Foods, phone (09) 261 1926

Chianti

'Key-ant-ee'

Italy's most famous offering to the wine world, though now being usurped by some sensational southern Italian reds. Chianti comes from the region of the same name, and for decades has been providing wine drinkers with interesting, savoury, earthy but still fruit-forward wines – all of which taste great with foods that have similar flavours, such as mushrooms, salamis, prosciutto, great ham and virtually any type of pasta.

The key to great chianti is that it can often be relatively acidic, making it a great with-food red wine. The following list grows slightly each year; none of the wines are packaged any longer in their stereotypical wicker baskets but they all provide good drinking.

Star chianti

2007 Piccini Chianti

$16–18 ☆☆☆½

2006 Bolla Chianti $18–19 ☆☆☆½

Brand new to New Zealand, the Bolla range of wines is quintessentially Italian in style, flavour and its ability to taste instantly good with food. I really like this soft, savoury, supple red.

Glengarry stores in the North Island and specialist wine stores nationwide

2006 Cecchi Chianti $18–19 ☆☆☆½

Once one of the best-known 'international' wine styles in New Zealand, chianti is now one of a growing range of often good-value European reds in this country. This version is a soft, spicy, bone-dry Italian red – it tastes good with a big bowl of midweek pasta.

🛒 Glengarry stores in the North Island and specialist wine stores nationwide

Star chianti

2007 Piccini Chianti

$16–18 ☆☆☆½

Its distinct orange label makes this big-production Tuscan chianti stand out from the crowd. Made mostly from sangiovese, it has dried cherry flavours with a savoury finish – drink with midweek meaty pasta in winter.

🛒 Specialist wine stores or Prodotti d'Italia, phone (09) 276 7140 or www.pdi.co.nz

2005 Piccini Chianti Riserva $21–22 ☆☆☆½

This is an intense, ripe chianti, one that offers very good quality.

🛒 Supermarkets, wine stores or for stockists contact Prodotti d'Italia, phone (09) 276 7140 or www.pdi.co.nz

2004 Piccini Riserva Chianti Selezione Oro Riserva
$24–25 ☆☆☆½

Robust, earthy chianti riserva that needs decanting prior to drinking – and also a hearty, slow-cooked winter casserole to go with it. Drink soon.

🛒 Supermarkets, wine stores or for stockists contact Prodotti d'Italia, phone (09) 276 7140 or www.pdi.co.nz

2006 Ruffino Chianti DOCG $16–17 ☆☆☆

Like many chiantis, this one is far more savoury in flavour than the so-called 'new world' reds of New Zealand and Australia, which Kiwis are more accustomed to. Earthy, spicy and slightly rustic, this wine tastes best with a bowl of pasta of your choice.

🛒 Specialist wine stores and A Touch of Italy, phone (09) 273 3701

Côtes-du-Rhône

'Coat-doo-Roan'

If you have yet to discover the incredible value for money that is the world of delicious under-$20 Côtes-du-Rhône, you need just two things: a $20 note (expect change) and the willingness to hotfoot it to your nearest specialist wine store. Every place worth going has at least one decent bottle of Côtes-du-Rhône available.

Of all the red wines available in New Zealand, the following bunch were in one of the most satisfying categories of the under-$20 in tastings held earlier this year (the only other such interesting category being Spain, but that's another story).

The Côtes-du-Rhône is in the southern part of France's Rhône Valley, a place where grenache rules the vineyards and is supplemented in the wines with smaller amounts of fascinating-tasting syrah (aka shiraz), carignan and cinsault. The result is a range of wines that taste warm, soft, spicy and light – and don't cost a bomb. If you drink red wine then these are must-tries, and if you don't, these are the sort of wines that could turn your preference away from white wine for ever due to their sheer drinkability and easy-to-like style.

Star Côtes-du-Rhône

2005 M Chapoutier Côtes-du-Rhône Belleruche

$20–21 ☆☆☆½

2006 Jaboulet Côtes-du-Rhône Parallèle 45 $21–22 ☆☆☆½

Of all the low-priced red wines in the world, Côtes-du-Rhône reds represent some of the most characterful, easiest to drink and best value for money. It's a combination of their soft tannins, light fruity style and smooth finish. They taste great with antipasto too.

🛒 Glengarry stores in the North Island and specialist wine stores nationwide

2005 Jaboulet Côtes du Ventoux Les Traverses $19–20 ☆☆☆½

Like its big brother, above, this is a lovely, soft, savoury French red. Great for everyday drinking, especially in winter.

🛒 Glengarry stores in the North Island and specialist wine stores nationwide

Star Côtes-du-Rhône

2005 M Chapoutier Côtes-du-Rhône Belleruche

$20–21 ☆☆☆½

Is it the Braille label, the fact that this French winery has turned the taste of its wines around by going biodynamic, or simply the fact that this soft, cheeky little red is such great value for money? I love the spicy, earthy taste of this good Côtes-du-Rhône, coupled with its fresh fruitiness.

🛒 Specialist wine stores

Dolcetto

'Doll-cheto'

2007 Brown Brothers Dolcetto Syrah $15–16 ☆☆☆

Unlikely combination of Italian and French grapes from the Brown Brothers winery in northern Victoria, Australia. To describe this wine as off-dry is pushing the limits a fair bit; it's definitely sweet in taste and style – and light – and made to appeal to new wine drinkers.

🛒 Widely available

Garnacha/grenache

'Gar-nash-a' or 'gren-ash'

Garnacha is its Spanish name, but in Australia and New Zealand this grape and the wines made from it are usually referred to as grenache, the French name for the world's second most-planted grape variety. Garnacha/grenache vines occupy vast tracts of vineyard land in Spain and southern France. In both places, garnacha and grenache express themselves with more oomph, power and weight than most versions of wines made from the grape grown elsewhere. Garnacha/grenache is also an important and delicious blending grape in the Rhône Valley, France.

As for the notion, suggested by some wine friends, that garnacha or grenache is not to be taken too seriously, I can only add that it tastes too good to be dismissed – and not only at a great-value, low-price level, either.

Now that the Spanish wine industry is making such massive strides to increase both the quality and the quantity of its wines, we may all start to refer to this grape by both its Spanish and its French names.

Read on and check out the star ratings of the following wines to get your tastebuds around some of the best-value reds in this book and available in New Zealand under $25.

Wine of the year
Star garnacha of the year

2006 Armantes Old Bush Vine Garnacha

$17–$19 ☆☆☆☆½

This is a great wine. Dark in colour, richly fruity in taste but bone dry, it tastes delicious now and history shows that it ages well too, provided you're keeping it in a cool, dark spot. Armantes is a range of mountains in Spain, where 50-year-old garnacha (aka grenache) grapes are grown at a high altitude. Master of Wine Steve Bennett and Matt Deller import it to New Zealand, introducing Kiwis to a world of other wine flavours. Needless to say, it is great value — and I chose it as my wine of the year for its wide appeal to all wine drinkers.

🛒 Specialist wine stores or contact Bennett & Deller for stockists near you, phone (09) 378 9463

2005 Hardys Oomoo McLaren Vale Grenache Shiraz Mourvedre

$16–18 ☆☆☆½ Screwcap

Ever tasted a red wine which really did deliver 'hints of chocolate' aroma and flavour? Here's one to blow your preconceptions — all that lovely, luscious grenache coupled with the richness of shiraz and mourvedre's dark chocolatey flavours . . . a very drinkable big red.

🛒 Widely available

2006 Jacob's Creek Grenache Shiraz $10–12 ☆☆☆ Screwcap

Light, soft, fruity everyday Australian red. A good lunchtime wine in the weekends or for a day at the beach.

🛒 Widely available

2004 Torres Sangre de Toro Grenache $19–20 ☆☆☆½

It's no surprise to find great grenache coming from Spain, where it is one of the most important red grapes, equally capable of making fruity everyday reds as it is of producing stellar top reds that can age and improve for decades. This fruity, earthy, everyday red is good value.

Specialist wine stores

Malbec

'Mal-beck'

Malbec, once all but obscure to everyone but winemakers who blended it with other red grapes, is now growing in stature, in our mindset and in plantings everywhere from Cahors in southwest France (where it was traditionally better known as 'Cot') to Argentina, Australia, New Zealand and Chile. Its biggest claim to fame today, both as cheap and cheerful reds and as top-notch reds, is in Argentina.

Star malbec

2005 Trapiche Broquel Malbec

$19–20 ☆☆☆½

2004 Kew Patutahi Malbec $18–20 ☆☆☆½

If you love big, robust reds, here's a wine to wake you up. Made from the Malbec grape, most famous in Argentina, it is a firm, tannined Kiwi red made with grapes grown in Gisborne.

Specialist wine stores

Star malbec

2005 Trapiche Broquel Malbec

$19–20 ☆☆☆½

This is a big, gutsy Argentinian red made from that country's most widely planted red grape, malbec. It offers firm tannins and rich, dark fruit flavours. Drink it with slow-cooked beef casserole or great steak on the BBQ.

🛒 Specialist wine stores

2007 Trapiche Mendoza Malbec $14–15 ☆☆☆☆ Screwcap

What an amazing difference to the freshness, cleanness and all-round bright fruit flavours of this wine. I love its tight acids, which support the robust big fruit flavours of the malbec grape well. This is a great BBQ wine or even good at a dinner party with some hearty, slow-cooked wild meat.

🛒 Liquor stores, specialist wine stores and some supermarkets

2005 Trapiche Oak Cask Malbec $15–16 ☆☆☆½

This is a big wine in every way but price. Its body, intense fruity flavours and spicy oak all add to its broad appeal as a good-value everyday red wine. It is easily robust enough to stand up to the juiciest steak you can muster.

🛒 Widely available

Merlot

'Mer-low'

Merlot has fallen off its perch of late, mostly because of the hit movie *Sideways*, which shifted pinot noir into prime position and relegated merlot to ABM (Anything But Merlot – as the movie's nerdy protagonist, Miles, famously stated). But that is only because many low-priced merlots have been undervalued owing to grapes being treated to high cropping levels and simplistic winemaking techniques that have shown merlot up to be a light fruit bomb at best. Nothing could be further from the truth.

Merlot is from Bordeaux, France, where it is more widely planted than cabernet sauvignon because it does provide precisely those fruity, appealing flavours, and also much more body. The best wines here hint at what merlot is capable of when it is good.

Star merlot

2006 Preece Merlot

$18–20 ☆☆☆☆

2005 Askerne Hawke's Bay Merlot Cabernet $20–21 ☆☆☆

Four different grapes go into this wine, the main two being merlot and cabernet sauvignon, with smaller amounts of malbec and cabernet franc adding sweet, rich, fruit and spice flavours. It's a dark-coloured Hawke's Bay red for everyday drinking; good with slow-roasted beef in wine.

Specialist wine stores or www.askerne.co.nz

2006 Bach 22 Merlot $13–14 ☆☆☆ Screwcap

It's not just the name of this wine that is quintessentially Kiwi. This is a soft, berry-tasting New Zealand merlot made for everyday drinking. Good value at this price – even better value if you find it for less.

Widely available

2005 Brown Brothers Victoria Merlot $18–19 ☆☆☆½ Screwcap

If you're a merlot lover, then take a bottle of this soft, fruity, everyday Australian red to your next BBQ.

Widely available

2006 Church Road Hawke's Bay Merlot $24–25 ☆☆☆½ Screwcap

Great-value merlot, which demonstrates just how far Hawke's Bay has come in the last half-decade. Fruit driven, spicy, nicely balanced and good value.

Widely available

2005 Commissioner's Block Merlot $15–16 ☆☆☆½ Screwcap

Merlot may be one of the last things that springs to mind where Australian reds are concerned, but here is one that provides very nice everyday drinking. Its bright fresh berry flavours couple nicely with zingy acids that add a food-friendly quality.

Widely available or www.robertsestatewines.com.au

2005 Corbans Private Bin Hawke's Bay Merlot Cabernet Sauvignon $22–23 ☆☆☆ Screwcap

This is a simple everyday red made from merlot and cabernet sauvignon grapes grown in Hawke's Bay. Always clean, fresh and well made, it has aromas and flavours of spice, berryfruit and a soft finish.

Widely available

2006 Crawford Farm Merlot $19–20 ☆☆☆½ Screwcap

This merlot is accessibly priced and made – its mouthfeel and texture are soft and easy to enjoy. Team up with slow-cooked casseroles to bring out the best in this wine.

🛒 Widely available or www.crawfordfarm.co.nz

2006 Drylands Marlborough Merlot $18–20 ☆☆☆½ Screwcap

Like the entire Drylands wine range, this merlot is a step up from many others in its price range – clean, bright berry flavours are delivered in a lingering tasty red wine. It's definitely a cut above most Kiwi merlots under $20.

🛒 Widely available

2006 Esk Valley Hawke's Bay Merlot $23–24 ☆☆☆½ Screwcap

One of the best New Zealand reds under $25 at the moment. Big, bold, fresh and spicy with lots of oak and fruit, this wine is very young right now and will reward a couple of years in the cellar or a couple of hours in the decanter prior to drinking.

🛒 Widely available

2006 Esk Valley Hawke's Bay Merlot Cabernet Sauvignon Malbec $23–24 ☆☆☆½ Screwcap

A more robust sibling of the wine above, this red features cabernet sauvignon and malbec in this three-way blend. It's big bodied – full of fresh, spicy and cedary oak flavours. Will also reward time in the bottle before opening or in the decanter prior to drinking.

🛒 Widely available

2006 Goldridge Estate Hawke's Bay Premium Reserve Merlot Cabernet $24–25 ☆☆☆ Screwcap

Like most New Zealand merlot-based reds, this one has soft fruity flavours with a tinge of herbs on the finish. It's a sound everyday red; better with food.

🛒 Specialist wine stores

2007 Goldridge Estate Hawke's Bay Premium Reserve Merlot Cabernet $24–25 ☆☆☆ Screwcap

This is not a double entry with the wine above, but rather a different vintage. Fresher, more fruity and upfront than the 2006, I prefer this wine. It has a slightly herby finish too, which could make it a good match with slow-cooked beef with lots of garden herbs thrown in.

🛒 Specialist wine stores

2006 Hardys Nottage Hill Merlot $10–12 ☆☆☆

Simple, light, everyday red made from merlot. Good value for a party or BBQ.

🛒 Widely available

2007 Hay Maker Hawke's Bay Merlot $19–20 ☆☆☆ Screwcap

This is a simple Kiwi merlot with sweet berry flavours and a dryish finish.

🛒 Liquor stores and specialist wine stores

2006 Huntaway Gisborne/Hawke's Bay Merlot Cabernet $18–20 ☆☆☆ Screwcap

A light, soft red wine made with grapes grown in Gisborne and Hawke's Bay. Has a few extra bells and whistles in flavour from oak and the judicious blending of grapes from two North Island regions.

🛒 Widely available

2005 Jacob's Creek Reserve Merlot $18–19 ☆☆☆☆ Screwcap

Big, bold, Australian merlot with intense dark, sweet berry flavours.

🛒 Widely available

2004 Kew Estate Merlot Gisborne $17–18 ☆☆☆½ Screwcap

One year older than the wine below, this merlot is fruity and berry flavoured. Ready to drink now, preferably with hearty, slow-cooked meat dishes in mid-winter.

🛒 Specialist wine stores or email info@kew.co.nz

2005 Kew Estate Merlot Gisborne $17–18 ☆☆☆½ Screwcap

Gisborne is better known for top white wines than for its reds, but this merlot is a good example of what the region can do with structured red wines. It's dark in colour with full body and fresh berry flavours.

🛒 Specialist wine stores or email info@kew.co.nz

2006 Laroche Merlot $19–20 ☆☆☆½ Screwcap

This soft southern French merlot has hints of spicy flavours and oak that intermingle with fresh berry fruit.

🛒 Glengarry stores in the North Island and specialist wine stores nationwide

2006 Longridge Hawke's Bay Merlot Cabernet Sauvignon $14–16 ☆☆☆½ Screwcap

Hawke's Bay and Kiwi reds have both come a long way this millennium, which is how this soft, easy-to-drink everyday red makes it in here. I like the spicy overtones and fresh fruit-driven style.

🛒 Widely available

2006 Maimai Creek Hawke's Bay Merlot $16–18 ☆☆☆ Screwcap

A very oak-driven merlot from Hawke's Bay. Reasonable as a glass before dinner but better value and flavours in red wines are easy to come by.

🛒 Online at www.maimaicreek.co.nz

2006 Mission Reserve Cabernet Merlot $19–20 ☆☆☆½

Once the most planted red grape in New Zealand, cabernet has been left in the dust of pinot noir and syrah, but it still makes a good everyday table wine – such as this lovely, lively, berry fruity blend.

🛒 Widely available

2006 Mission Vineyard Selection Mere Road Merlot
$22–24 ☆☆☆½ Screwcap

Like most of the wines in Mission Estate's 'Vineyard Selection' range, this is an outstanding one in terms of flavour and value for money. Soft, sensuous merlot berryfruit combine with a hint of savoury, even earthy notes. Really good value for everyday satisfaction.

🛒 Widely available

2006 Moana Park Gimblett Road Merlot Malbec
$24–25 ☆☆☆½ Screwcap

The combination of soft, fruity merlot with hearty, more tannic malbec makes for an interesting red wine with a strong personality. Drink with game food or your favourite barbecued meat, preferably done rare.

🛒 Specialist wine stores or www.moanapark.co.nz

2006 Montana Reserve Marlborough Merlot
$24–25 ☆☆☆ Screwcap

Even when good, Marlborough merlot is a simple fruity wine at best. This version is fresh and clean with raspberry flavours. Everyday drinking.

🛒 Widely available

2006 Montes Classic Merlot $19–20 ☆☆☆½

Soft, full-bodied merlot with lots of firm oak support adding spicy flavours and weight in the mouth. Good value for lovers of big meaty reds.

🛒 Glengarry stores in the North Island and specialist wine stores nationwide

2007 Mud House Hawke's Bay Merlot $19–20 ☆☆☆ Screwcap

Light, simple everyday red with a slight herbal edge. Drink at a BBQ.

🛒 Liquor stores and specialist wine stores

2006 Nobilo Hawke's Bay Merlot $12–13 ☆☆☆ Screwcap

A very light but easy-to-drink merlot made with grapes grown in Hawke's Bay. Good for an after-work glass or two, early in the week.

🛒 Widely available

2006 One Tree Hawke's Bay Merlot $20-21 ☆☆☆½

There are fresh berry flavours in every sip of this soft, fruity merlot from Hawke's Bay.

🛒 Specialist wine stores or www.craggyrange.com

2006 Pasqua Le Collezioni Merlot $13–14 ☆☆☆½

This is a simple, light-bodied red from Italy made from the merlot grape. Its flavours are of firm tannins, berryfruit and earthiness. Serve with tasty sausages on the BBQ.

🛒 Glengarry stores in the North Island and other specialist wine and liquor stores

2006 Piccini Merlot Syrah $15–16 ☆☆☆

A slightly rustic Sicilian red wine – good drinking with a bowl of meaty, spicy midweek pasta.

🛒 Supermarkets, wine stores or for stockists contact Prodotti d'Italia, phone (09) 276 7140 or www.pdi.co.nz

Star merlot

2006 Preece Merlot

$18–20 ☆☆☆☆ Screwcap

Like the rest of the Preece range, this merlot is great value for money – soft, but also robust in the mid-palate, offering surprising body and flavour.

🛒 Liquor stores and specialist wine stores

2006 Rongopai Seasonal Merlot $14–15 ☆☆☆ Screwcap

This New Zealand merlot is made with grapes grown on the East Coast of the North Island. It's a medium-bodied red with flavours of berries and spice. Decant, if possible, for an hour or two before drinking.

🛒 New World and Pak'nSave

2006 Roy's Hill Merlot Cabernet $20–22 ☆☆☆½ Screwcap

A good everyday New Zealand red from Hawke's Bay, home to the best merlot and cabernet sauvignon grapes in this country. Drink with your favourite steak.

🛒 Widely available

2006 Sandalford Element Merlot $16–17 ☆☆☆½ Screwcap

If you've ever wondered why merlot is often compared to fresh berries, try this easy-drinking everyday Australian version. It has dark fruit flavours lending themselves to a round-the-fire glass or two. Good value for money.

Widely available

2006 Selaks Hawke's Bay Merlot $16–17 ☆☆☆ Screwcap

A simple light red made from merlot. Treat it as a BBQ beverage or for everyday drinking.

Widely available

2004 Shipwreck Bay Merlot Cabernet $18–20 ☆☆☆ Screwcap

It has a good price, a screwcap and an appealing label, but this is definitely an everyday wine rather than one for a special occasion. Simple, light and reasonable for a quick midweek glass.

Online at www.okahuestate.co.nz

2006 Stoneleigh Marlborough Merlot $16–17 ☆☆☆ Screwcap

It's the taste of spicy, savoury oak that adds another dimension to this slightly light Marlborough merlot. This wine offers very decent value from New Zealand's largest wine region, which is no mean feat at this price and for merlot from Marlborough.

Widely available

2005 Thornbury Marlborough Merlot $20–21 ☆☆☆ Screwcap

Ready to drink now, this Kiwi merlot is best reserved for everyday drinking with meaty, wintery food.

Widely available

2006 Timara Oak Aged Merlot $12–14 ☆☆☆ Screwcap

A light, simple red with flavour interest derived from spicy oak integration. Everyday red for a BBQ or week night.

Widely available

2006 Villa Maria Cellar Selection Merlot Cabernet Sauvignon $24–25 ☆☆☆☆ Screwcap

Its gold label is apt on this Hawke's Bay blend of merlot and cabernet sauvignon, where quality and everyday drinking meet face to face. This is a robust, big and ripe-tasting Kiwi red wine.

Widely available

2006 Villa Maria Private Bin Hawke's Bay Merlot $17–18 ☆☆☆ Screwcap

Good everyday New Zealand merlot, with big, rounded tannins and lots of upfront, fruity flavours.

Widely available

2006 Windmill Te Awa Merlot Cabernet $20–21 ☆☆☆ Screwcap

It might be an old-fashioned windmill that adorns the label on this bottle, but the wine inside is a modern merlot every bit of the way. Made from grapes grown in the Gimblett Gravels district of Hawke's Bay, it is a nicely balanced blend of merlot and cabernet sauvignon – berries and spice intermingle.

Widely available

2005 Wishart Te Puriri Merlot $18–20 ☆☆☆ Screwcap

Like most New Zealand wineries, Wishart is small, but the quality of this merlot is surprisingly high – berry flavours are held together in a fresh, clean style.

Specialist wine stores

2005 Wyndham Estate Bin 999 Merlot $16–17 ☆☆☆½

If value is half the reason for this book (which it must be), then this wine gains some of its appeal on price. Still a pretty basic drop, it is better value than many others at a couple of dollars more. Drink at a BBQ.

Widely available

2006 Zilzie Merlot $18–19 ☆☆☆

This is a soft, simple Australian merlot – lots of oak adds the impression of richness and full body.

Specialist wine stores

Monastrell

'Moe-nah-strell'

2006 Carchelo $16–17 ☆☆☆½

Classic, soft, young Spanish red, made from monastrell (mourvedre) and syrah – great with hearty meat, slow-cooked or barbecued, and also with tasty cheeses, which match its earthy flavours.

Liquor stores and specialist wine stores

2006 Carchelo Monastrell Syrah Tinto $16–17 ☆☆☆½

It's well known, it's Spanish and it's a great-value everyday red. Dense, dark and flavoursome, this plummy rich red offers lots of interest at a great price.

Liquor stores and specialist wine stores

2004 Hecula Monastrell Castano $18–20 ☆☆☆½

Interesting, great-value Spanish red made in a clean and fresh, upfront fruity style with lots of layers of savoury, earthy flavours. This wine has all the weight and density of a good Australian red, but has the earthy flavours that show it is clearly a European wine.

Online at www.wineimporter.co.nz

2004 Montgo Monastrell Shiraz Yecla $20 ☆☆☆☆

This is a robust, big, easy-to-love wintery red wine with fresh acids that add lively character. Powerful and impressive. Imported by The Wine Importer, who is also known as Paul Mitchell, in West Auckland.

Online at www.wineimporter.co.nz

Montepulciano

'Mon-tee-pull-che-arn-o'

Montepulciano is a grape and also a Renaissance hill town in southern Tuscany, Italy. The grape is also known as cordisco, morellone, primaticcio and uva Abruzzi. Montepulciano, the town, is 605 metres above sea level (around 2000 feet) and sits on a high limestone ridge, 124 kilometres southeast of Florence and 186 kilometres north of Rome.

The grape and the wine made from it are what this chapter is all about, and there are more of them available in New Zealand each year. Most montepulcianos are in the under-$25 price range, representing great value for money.

Star montepulciano

2007 Valle Reale Vigne Nuove Montepulciano

$22–23 ☆☆☆☆

2006 Canaletto Montepulciano d'Abruzzo

$19–20 ☆☆☆☆ Screwcap

The Canaletto range of reds from Italy provide not only great value for money, but also outstanding 'different' wines such as this soft, sensuous and spicy-tasting montepulciano.

Specialist wine stores or for stockists contact Prodotti d'Italia, phone (09) 276 7140 or www.pdi.co.nz

2005 Farnese Farneto Valley Montepulciano d'Abruzzo
$18–20 ☆☆☆

This montepulciano is a good, everyday, entry-level Italian red with light fruit flavours coupled with a characteristic Italian grapey-earthy aroma and taste.

Specialist wine stores or contact A Touch of Italy, phone (09) 273 3701

2005 Morton Estate Montepulciano $19–20 ☆☆☆ Screwcap

Why is montepulciano made in New Zealand so darned hard to find? Simply because few wineries have yet delved into growing Italian grapes, particularly because it is not as warm here as in Italy, which has more of a continental climate. This is a light, slightly spicy, simple red wine – good daytime drinking.

Specialist wine stores or contact Morton Estate, phone (09) 300 5050 or email fionam@mortonestatewines.co.nz

2006 Pasqua Le Collezioni Montepulciano $12–13 ☆☆☆

Like the other montepulcianos in this chapter, this is a soft, smooth, Italian red that is easy to enjoy – great value for everyday drinking.

Glengarry stores in the North Island and specialist wine stores nationwide

2006 Pasqua Montepulciano Terre del Sole
$12–13 ☆☆☆½

Renamed, repackaged and more popular than ever before, this Italian red wine retains at least one element of its past – it is great value for money for such fresh, fruit-driven and savoury flavours.

Glengarry stores in the North Island and specialist wine stores nationwide

Star montepulciano

2007 Valle Reale Vigne Nuove Montepulciano

$22–23 ☆☆☆☆

To describe this wine as great value for money is to wildly understate just how modern but still quintessentially Italian it is. Big ripe fruit flavours lead the palate here; it has lots of depth of flavour, body and balance.

🛒 Specialist wine stores or contact Bennett & Deller for stockists near you, phone (09) 378 9463

Negroamaro

'Neg-row am-are-oh'

Negroamaro (also known as negro amaro) is one of the most prolific grape varieties planted in Italy, most notably in the south and particularly in Apulia. The wines it makes are characterised by fleshy texture and rounded, sweet, ripe, fruity flavours with savoury spice aromas. They are always good value for money.

Star negroamaro

2006 Menhir NZero Negroamaro

$20 ☆☆☆½

Southern Italian red made from the fruity, soft, deliciously robust negroamaro grape. This is outstanding value for money.

Specialist wine stores or contact Bennett & Deller for stockists near you, phone (09) 378 9463

2004 Terriero Negroamaro $14–15 ☆☆☆½ –☆☆☆☆

It's easy to see why this wine won a gold medal – and scores consistently highly in this guide. The label may hark back to old-fashioned Italy, but this is a modern, fruit-led wine with interesting spicy flavours. If this is what Puglia tastes like, bring it on!

Wine stores or for stockists contact Prodotti d'Italia, phone (09) 276 7140 or www.pdi.co.nz

Nero d'avola

'Neh-roe dah-voe-lah'

Inspiring, beautiful, delicious and rustic, by turns, Sicily is home to nearly six million Italians, some of the best seafood in the world and captivatingly delicious red wines such as nero d'avola. This grape is also known as calabrese, suggesting that it might have originated on Italy's mainland in Calabria.

There is a growing number of fantastic-tasting nero d'avolas available in New Zealand, and all are great value, offering lithe, smooth texture and masses of spicy flavours, derived both from the grape itself and from the oak that nero d'avola wines are usually matured in.

Star nero d'avolas (double winners)

2006 Corallo Nero d'Avola Sicilia $10–12 ☆☆☆☆

2006 La Mura Nero d'Avola $14–15 ☆☆☆☆

2005 Canaletto Nero d'Avola Merlot $19–20 ☆☆☆☆

This massive, big, soft red from Sicily speaks volumes about warm-climate red wine. It has hints of shiraz fruitiness, spanning the gamut of soft, peachy floral flavours through to firm backbone and a lingering taste on the finish. It is definitely big enough to satisfy those looking for shiraz-styled wines.

Wine stores or for stockists contact Prodotti d'Italia, phone (09) 276 7140 or www.pdi.co.nz

2005 Cavallina Nero d'Avola Syrah IGT $15–16 ☆☆☆½ Screwcap

If you haven't heard of nero d'avola, you are far from alone, but this is one of the wine world's greatest-value red wines. Indigenous to Sicily, it's a fantastically soft, fruity and lightly spicy red wine, beautifully rounded in body and velvety in texture. Just fabulous value.

Sovrano, Auckland, phone (09) 271 5969

Star nero d'avolas (double winners)

2006 Corallo Nero d'Avola Sicilia

$10–12 ☆☆☆☆ Screwcap

In another 10 years, if not before, this soft, fruity, indigenous Sicilian red wine will soon be a fave with red wine lovers. It's savoury and spicy but mostly just a darned good drink. Soft, smooth tannins – a sort of Sicilian beaujolais.

Wine Direct, Newmarket, Auckland, in store or www.winedirect.co.nz

2006 La Mura Nero d'Avola

$14–15 ☆☆☆☆ Screwcap

How much can one modern, low-priced and delicious wine have going for it? This Sicilian nero d'avola is too easy to love, but it is not reflective of shiraz in a style sense. It has great appeal for anyone who loves European red wine, or who is new to red wine. It's lighter than shiraz in taste and body, and makes a great introduction to what good-quality, modern European dry red wine is all about. It's also one of Sicily's first screwcapped wines.

Wine stores or for stockists contact Prodotti d'Italia, phone (09) 276 7140 or www.pdi.co.nz

Other Italian reds

Italy may not be large in land mass, but it is one of the biggest wine producers in the world – and definitely the most varied. Where New Zealand has just 17 different grape varieties in common usage, Italy has over 400. Italians are passionate about cultivating every available square inch of land in viticulture and horticulture, and today they are on a path to revive old, forgotten grape varieties, often in new areas of their vinous country.

Star other Italian red

2007 Tegole Piccini Toscana IGT

$16–18 ☆☆☆☆

2006 Cecchi La Mora Morellino Di Scansano $18–20 ☆☆☆☆

From Maremma, the hottest part of Tuscany – literally and figuratively speaking – comes this fresh, new-wave Italian red that successfully straddles both an old Italy, savoury-styled red and a bright, fresh, fruity wine.

🛒 Glengarry stores in the North Island and specialist wine stores nationwide

2006 Piccini Solco $19–20 ☆☆☆½

This Italian red is best summed up as soft, smooth and velvety. It's an everyday red, yes, but it offers surprisingly complex flavours of spice, earth and fruit. Great value.

🛒 Specialist wine stores or for stockists contact Prodotti d'Italia, phone (09) 276 7140 or www.pdi.co.nz

2006 Remole Toscana Frescobaldi $18–20 ☆☆☆½

This is a great-value Tuscan red wine, made from sangiovese combined with cabernet sauvignon. It's a modern Italian style, and very good value for different, interesting flavours. Great with pizza.

🛒 Widely available in specialist wine stores and some supermarkets

Star other Italian red

2007 Tegole Piccini Toscana IGT

$16–18 ☆☆☆☆

This instantly likeable Tuscan wine is soft, gentle and fruity – a great expression of the sangiovese grape that commands your attention here, from the first whiff of savoury-sweet Italian wine to the last, lingering sip. Four stars for sure – this is great value.

🛒 Specialist wine stores or for stockists contact Prodotti d'Italia, phone (09) 276 7140 or www.pdi.co.nz

Other New Zealand reds

2004 Trinity Hill Hawke's Bay Trinity $19–20 ☆☆☆½ Screwcap

It's actually trinity plus one, this red blend of merlot, cabernet franc, cabernet sauvignon and syrah. This is a really successful blend of these four grapes, which marry beautifully together here to make a spicy, fruit-driven, multi-layered red wine. I love its fresh, bright, pure fruitiness and lingering finish.

🛒 Specialist wine stores or www.trinityhill.com

2005 Trinity Hill Hawke's Bay Trinity $19–20 ☆☆☆½ Screwcap

A younger version than the 2004 (above), proving that age works wonders even on red wines of this price, softening and mellowing them. This is also good, but save it a year or two and watch it chill out into an even more drinkable red.

🛒 Specialist wine stores or www.trinityhill.com

Other Spanish reds

2003 Chivite Gran Feudo Reserva $25 ☆☆☆☆

From family-owned Bodegas Chivite in Spain comes this soft, delicious Spanish blend of tempranillo, cabernet sauvignon and merlot. It's a successful combination of two new-wave grapes in Spain plus the early-ripening tempranillo, which adds a silky smooth and quintessentially Spanish taste to the wine. This winery was founded in 1647, modernised in 1990 and is run today by four Chivites: Julián, Carlos, Fernando and Mercedes.

Fine Wine Delivery Company and other specialist wine stores or contact Bennett & Deller for stockists near you, phone (09) 378 9463

Pinotage

'Pee-no-tazh'

Pinotage was formed in South Africa in 1925 by crossing pinot noir with cinsault. The result is pinotage, an early-ripening, hardy grape. It is grown widely in South Africa and used to be popular in New Zealand with winemakers and drinkers alike, but has now declined in plantings, popularity and general appeal. It is grown in few other places in the world.

2005 Soljans Estate Pinotage $18–19 ☆☆☆½ Screwcap

Fresh and fruity pinotage with berry and spice flavours. A simple but pleasant late-afternoon wine.

Super Liquor or www.soljans.co.nz

Pinot noir

'Pee-no nwa'

Pinot noir is on a roll. In the last 10 years it has grown from a measly 400-odd hectares planted in New Zealand's vineyards to more than 5000 hectares – and it's still snowballing nationwide. Pinot noir has even eclipsed chardonnay, with which it tied as the second most planted grape in this country a year ago, and is also this country's most planted red grape. While it is extremely easy to pronounce, easy to love and popular, pinot noir is a thin-skinned grape, hence it's a difficult grape to grow – and a difficult wine to make.

Pinot noir is the famous red of Burgundy, France, where its greatest expression is the famous DRC – Domaine de la Romanée-Conti – which is rare, restrained, made in tiny quantities and fantastically good. However, there are a few places other than Burgundy in which pinot noir expresses itself well, notably Oregon in the United States, some parts of the Yarra Valley in Australia, and Central Otago, Marlborough, Waipara and the Wairarapa in New Zealand.

For many wine fanatics, any pinot noir but burgundy is a pretender, but this grape is now both more widely produced and in better forms around the world than ever before. The cheaper wines are generally pale versions of top-notch pinot noir, but those with three stars and above show great potential for the future.

Star pinot noir

2006 Montana Reserve Pinot Noir

$24–25 ☆☆☆½

2006 Canaletto Autentico Italiano Pinot Noir

$12–14 ☆☆☆ Screwcap

Very light, fresh, cherry-flavoured pinot noir from Italy. A simple red wine that is unrelentingly dry – a positive. Good for newcomers to wine but definitely not in the category of big shiraz-styled reds.

Specialist wine stores or for stockists contact Prodotti d'Italia, phone (09) 276 7140 or www.pdi.co.nz

2006 Cape Campbell Marlborough Pinot Noir

$24–25 ☆☆☆½ Screwcap

From New Zealand's largest wine region comes this vibrant, fruity, cherry-tasting pinot noir. Good everyday drinking – even better with game meats.

Online at www.capecampbell.co.nz

2007 Crawford Farm Pinot Noir

$20–22 ☆☆☆ Screwcap

This evocatively-labelled new pinot noir is a good everyday drop; very light and pretty in a floral style. It's an easy wine for BBQs and parties, or take it to the beach.

Widely available

2006 Forrest Estate Marlborough Pinot Noir

$19–20 ☆☆☆½ Screwcap

Like most pinot noirs at this price, this big-namer is soft, light and fruity with hints of savoury, gamey, earthy flavours. Good value for a light, clean, fruity introduction to pinot noir.

🛒 Widely available in liquor stores and good supermarkets or www.forrestwines.co.nz

2006 Goldridge Estate Marlborough Premium Reserve Pinot Noir $24–25 ☆☆☆½ Screwcap

Good everyday pinot noir with rich, toasty oak intermingling with sweet cherry and berryfruit flavours.

🛒 Specialist wine stores

2006 Kaituna Valley Canterbury Pinot Noir $22–23 ☆☆☆½ Screwcap

It's light, cherry-like in flavour and so soft that you'll want more than one glass of this pure, fresh, southern Kiwi pinot noir. This is great value and a lovely expression of very good everyday pinot noir.

🛒 Liquor stores and specialist wine stores

2007 Kim Crawford Marlborough Pinot Noir $18–20 ☆☆☆½ Screwcap

Winemaker Kim Crawford needs little or no introduction, but this pinot noir does. It's one of the best yet made under his famous label. Soft, cherry flavours team up with zingy acids to stretch out the flavours to a lingering finish. Good value.

🛒 Widely available

2007 King's Road Waipara Pinot Noir $23–24 ☆☆☆½ Screwcap

This is a big, fruit bomb of a pinot noir from Waipara in North Canterbury. With a hint of sweetness to fill out the mid-palate, this wine is a good-value everyday pinot noir.

🛒 Specialist wine stores

2006 Kono Marlborough Pinot Noir $16–18 ☆☆☆½ Screwcap

This is a very light, easy-to-drink Marlborough pinot noir with a suggested food match of duck, lamb or veal – anything gamey and strong will do the trick.

Specialist wine stores or www.kono-nz.com

2006 Lake Chalice Marlborough Pinot Noir
$22–24 ☆☆☆½ Screwcap

Here's more proof that Marlborough pinot noir is just getting better and better. Fresh, bright cherry flavours leap out of each glass of this vibrant red.

Specialist wine stores or www.lakechalice.com

2006 Main Divide Pinot Noir $19–20 ☆☆☆½ Screwcap

This wine is part of the famous Pegasus Bay wine stable, made with grapes grown around the South Island. Easily delivers in flavour, with a sweet, fruity style.

Specialist wine stores or www.maindivide.com

2006 Maven Marlborough Pinot Noir $24–25 ☆☆☆½ Screwcap

Like a great Beaujolais Villages wine, this lovely Marlborough pinot noir is chock-full of cherry and berry flavours. It's a light-styled red wine, great for everyday drinking – especially good with robust pasta dishes.

Specialist wine stores or www.mavenwines.co.nz

Star pinot noir

2006 Montana Reserve Pinot Noir

$24–25 ☆☆☆½ Screwcap

It may not be as easy elsewhere on the planet to find as good a pinot noir for value as this one, but thankfully, the largest wine company in New Zealand makes loads of this soft and supple pinot noir at this price while retaining its quality.

Widely available

2006 Mud House Central Otago Pinot Noir

$24–25 ☆☆☆½ Screwcap

This light pinot noir has deliciously juicy wine-gum flavours – a hallmark of Central Otago – and a savoury finish.

Widely available

2007 Mud House Marlborough Pinot Noir $24–25 ☆☆☆ Screwcap

Same winery but a different region to the pinot noir above, this one is a very simple and light red with off-dry fruity flavours. A good beginner's red.

Liquor stores and specialist wine stores

2005 Mystery Creek Reserve Pinot Noir $24–25 ☆☆☆ Screwcap

Some will find this wine appealing, but it is extremely light in taste, offering below-par value for money compared with the plethora of other pinot noirs at between $13 and $30 on the market right now. That said, it's clean and fresh, but just lacks intensity.

Specialist wine stores or www.mysterycreekwines.com

2006 Nobilo Icon Marlborough Pinot Noir

$23–24 ☆☆☆½ Screwcap

This stellar Marlborough pinot noir from the vast Nobilo winery is easily the star wine in the 'Icon' range. Fresh, bright and plummy, it offers really great value for money.

Widely available

2006 Opawa Marlborough Pinot Noir $19–20 ☆☆☆½ Screwcap

Opawa is Maori for 'smoky river', which is the name of the vineyard where the grapes in this wine were grown. This is soft, light and savoury in flavour – definitely best with food rather than without.

🛒 Liquor stores and specialist wine stores or email kironside@nautilusestate.com

2006 Renato Nelson Pinot Noir $24–25 ☆☆☆ Screwcap

This is an extremely light pinot noir, both in colour and flavour, but it's a good summertime drop when you need a fresh, simple red wine.

🛒 Specialist wine stores or www.renatoestate.co.nz

2006 Richmond Plains Nelson Pinot Noir $19–20 ☆☆☆½

Here's a lovely, Kiwi beaujolais-style pinot noir – full of fresh, red cherry flavours and a lively, lingering finish. Perfect lunchtime wine for its light style.

🛒 Specialist wine stores or email info@richmondplains.co.nz

2006 Rose Tree Cottage Marlborough Pinot Noir
$23–24 ☆☆☆½ Screwcap

This is a light, fresh Marlborough pinot noir with a little weight in the mid-palate to add flavour interest and depth.

🛒 Widely available

2006 Russian Jack Pinot Noir $24–25 ☆☆☆ Screwcap

From its great label to its light flavour, this is an appealing everyday pinot noir. The price may push your boundaries a little further, but this wine is definitely a week-night drop. If you're wondering about the name, Russian Jack was a famous swagger –

the name given to the early pioneers who cleared the Wairarapa scrub.

Online at www.burntspur.co.nz

2007 Saint Clair Marlborough Pinot Noir $19–20 ☆☆☆½ Screwcap

Light it may be, but this Marlborough pinot noir is a smooth, easy red that goes down all too easily on either a hot summer's afternoon at the beach or as an after-work drink in winter. Fresh, clean, simple cherry flavours make it a good introduction to red wine too.

Widely available

2007 Saint Clair Vicar's Choice Marlborough Pinot Noir
$16–17 ☆☆☆ Screwcap

Not sure who the vicar in question is other than a relative of the owners of Saint Clair Winery, but this pinot noir is easily one of the best value at its price. Soft and light, it tastes of fresh fruit.

Widely available

2006 Selaks Premium Selection Pinot Noir $14–16 ☆☆☆ Screwcap

This is a very light Kiwi pinot noir with hints of spice, fresh cherry fruit and a soft finish. It's a good introduction to red wine.

Widely available

2007 Sileni Cellar Selection Hawke's Bay Pinot Noir
$24–25 ☆☆☆ Screwcap

He might be better known for making merlot, but Hawke's Bay winemaker Grant Edmonds is nothing if not versatile – just like his wines. This is a very light pinot noir for everyday drinking, with or without food. Tastes soft and light, with hints of cherry flavour – a great BBQ wine.

Specialist wine stores or www.sileni.co.nz

2005 Southbank Estate Marlborough Pinot Noir $24–25 ☆☆☆

This is a light, soft pinot noir in a classy package, but with an everyday drinking style and quality.

Specialist wine stores

2006 Spinyback Nelson Pinot Noir $17–18 ☆☆☆½ Screwcap

This is a great value wine for its price; there are few pinot noirs at an accessible price point anywhere these days, and this soft, light but fruit-driven Nelson wine provides lovely flavour and outstanding value for money. For every bottle of Spinyback Pinot Noir that you buy, a five-cent donation goes towards education about the tuatara, New Zealand's 'living fossil'.

Specialist wine stores or www.waimeaestates.co.nz

2007 Stoneleigh Marlborough Pinot Noir
$18–20 ☆☆☆½ Screwcap

Even five years ago it was hard to come by pinot noirs in this price range, let alone one that tastes as good as this. Fresh, dry and fruity, this is merely an entrée to the world of pinot noir, but it's a subtle, fleshy, extremely enjoyable one.

Widely available

2006 Stone Paddock Central Otago Pinot Noir
$24–25 ☆☆☆½ Screwcap

This is a light, fresh and impressive everyday pinot noir, made with grapes grown in Central Otago. Hints of spice combine with the bright fruit flavours here.

Specialist wine stores or www.stonepaddock.com

2007 Taylors Adelaide Hills Pinot Noir $18–20 ☆☆☆½ Screwcap

Nothing stays still for long, and the Australians are now searching for cooler areas from which to make more subtle red wines, such as this impressive but light pinot noir. It's a very good everyday, beaujolais-like red. Great value at this price.

Widely available

2006 Te Mania Nelson Reserve Pinot Noir $22–24 ☆☆☆½

Here's a robust pinot noir for summertime drinking. Lots of firm tannins add a dimension of body to this Nelson wine, but it is more of a warm-weather red due to its innate light, spicy fruit flavours. Drink with good grana padano or tasty cheese, before dinner.

Specialist wine stores

2006 The Crossings Marlborough Pinot Noir
$18–20 ☆☆☆½ Screwcap

Proof that New Zealand pinot noir has come a long way in a short time comes in this form – light, bright and fresh, and great value to boot, so long as you treat this as an everyday wine.

Widely available or www.thecrossings.co.nz

2006 The Jibe Latitude 41 Pinot Noir $22–24 ☆☆☆ Screwcap

If you didn't immediately know that latitude 41 degrees south was Marlborough, then welcome to the region with this soft, fruity pinot noir. It's light and fresh – good everyday drinking.

Widely available or www.nobilo.co.nz

2007 The Ned Pinot Noir $24–25 ☆☆☆½ Screwcap

Five years ago it was almost impossible to find pinot noirs at this price that tasted so good. Soft, smooth, rich and plummy in style, it's made for drinking rather than cellaring. This wine is medium bodied but packed with flavour, so it will stand up well to your favourite meat cooked on the BBQ.

Widely available

2006 Trinity Hill Pinot Noir $19–20 ☆☆☆½ Screwcap

Hawke's Bay pinot noir might usually get a bad rap, but this spicy, big-bodied version puts paid to all the usual notions about it. I like the depth of fruit flavour in this wine, which marries well with the black pepper and savoury tastes here.

🛒 Trinity Hill cellar door, State Highway 50, Hastings, or www.trinityhill.com

2007 Twin Islands Marlborough Pinot Noir
$19–20 ☆☆☆½ Screwcap

Soft, smooth, great value and an easy drink too, this Marlborough pinot noir has the added bonus of being easy to find. Its flavours are of light, fresh cherries.

🛒 Widely available

2006 Vidal Marlborough Pinot Noir $24–25 ☆☆☆☆ Screwcap

This is a very good pinot noir from New Zealand's largest wine region. Bright, clean, fresh fruity flavours lead the way in this robust, medium-bodied red. Spicy flavours add interest to every sip.

🛒 Widely available

2006 Villa Maria Marlborough Pinot Noir $22–23 ☆☆☆½ Screwcap

Cherries, red plums and fresh soft tannins all combine to make this light pinot noir a lively everyday red.

🛒 Widely available

2007 Waipara Hills Marlborough Pinot Noir
$19–20 ☆☆☆½ Screwcap

Waipara Hills is a North Canterbury winery, but the grapes in this friendly little red number were actually grown in Marlborough. Soft, light and fresh – a tasty but simple everyday red.

🛒 Specialist wine stores

2006 Wairau River Marlborough Pinot Noir

$19–20 ☆☆☆½ Screwcap

Here's a surprise – a low-priced pinot noir with loads of flavour. It's the spicy, bright, fresh cherry aromas and flavours that taste so good here. It's a lighter style of pinot noir, but good value for money.

🛒 Widely available or www.wairauriverwines.com

2006 Wyndham Estate Bin 333 Pinot Noir $14–15 ☆☆☆ Screwcap

Passable Australian pinot noir, which is extremely light in flavour and body.

🛒 Widely available

Portuguese reds

If you're really lucky or good at finding needles in haystacks, you might just count on more than five fingers all the Portuguese red wines in New Zealand – table wines, we're talking, as opposed to port. Many very good, modern, great-value red table wines are made in Portugal today, and have been for decades, but they are far lower in profile than port, which is a shame given their high quality.

If you're a fan of big red wines, be sure to check out this relative newcomer to New Zealand.

2005 Barco Negro Douro Vindima Lurton $24–25 ☆☆☆☆

Here is a modern Portuguese red that will blow your preconceptions and tastebuds out of the water, without denting your budget at all. A strong contender for wine of the year, this has big, lush, rich fruit flavours that combine with lovely savoury overtones. Love it.

🛒 Specialist wine stores or contact Bennett & Deller Wine Merchants for stockists near you, phone (09) 378 9463

Primitivo

'Prim-it-ee-voh'

Primitivo is one of the top 10 most planted grapes in Italy, and is distantly related to the famously known and infamously sweet-tasting zinfandel, which is grown in North America as the red grape it is to produce 'white zin', a sweet, low-quality blush/rosé wine. Primitivo is planted in southern Italy and makes dark-coloured, richly sweet-tasting red wines that tend to have relatively high alcohol.

2006 Caleo Primitivo Salento $14–15 ☆☆☆½

This southern Italian primitivo is fresh, light and soft, with overt fruit sweetness to recommend it to shiraz lovers.

Specialist wine stores or for stockists contact Prodotti d'Italia, phone (09) 276 7140 or www.pdi.co.nz

Star primitivo

2004 Canaletto Primitivo

$19–20 ☆☆☆☆

A consistent winner in this wine guide for good reason. It is a big southern Italian red, driven more by savoury flavours than the characteristic sweet fruitiness of most shiraz – that said, it will garner a fan club, easily.

Specialist wine stores or for stockists contact Prodotti d'Italia, phone (09) 276 7140 or www.pdi.co.nz

2006 Pasqua Oak Aged Primitivo Salento $17–18 ☆☆☆☆

This oak-aged southern Italian red offers lots of depth, flavour and weight for everyday drinking. Its savoury flavours mean this wine comes into its own with food rather than without.

🛒 Glengarry stores and other specialist wine stores, including some supermarkets

2006 San Marzano Primitivo Puglia $16–17 ☆☆☆½

A gutsy southern Italian red made from primitivo, which has its home in Puglia – the 'heel' of the Italian 'boot'. Big, bold, and good with gamey food.

🛒 Sovrano, Auckland, phone (09) 271 5969

Rioja

'Rio-ka'

Spain's most famous red wine, based on the early ripening, silky smooth red tempranillo grape, but usually including noticeable proportions of garnacha and nearly always well acquainted with the insides of seasoned American oak barrels. At its apex, rioja can be one of the greatest wines in the world. At an everyday price, it offers great value for money for big, robust, red-wine drinking.

2006 Sierra Cantabria Rioja Cosecha $25 ☆☆☆☆

It might be three years old already, but this huge, fruity Spanish red still tastes incredibly youthful, which is great news for red-wine lovers, who will relish getting their lips around this wonderfully spicy, modern rioja. Needless to say, it's fantastic value for money.

🛒 Specialist wine stores or contact Bennett & Deller for stockists near you, phone (09) 378 9463

2004 Solar Viejo Crianza $16–18 ☆☆☆½

For a four-year-old red that's come from the other side of the planet at this price, this wine is fantastic value for money. Erring on the savoury, slightly rustic heartland Spanish style, it's a robust, hearty red packed with flavour.

🛒 Glengarry stores in the North Island and specialist wine stores nationwide

Sangiovese

'San-gee-oh-vay-see'

Sangiovese is both Italy's most famous and its least-known grape variety, because this is the main component in chianti. About 10 per cent of Italy's national vineyard area is planted in sangiovese, and while it has travelled to some other countries, few countries or wine regions outside of Tuscany grow significant amounts of it, with the notable exception of Australia. Quantities of sangiovese in Australia are still small, but are increasing in both quantity and quality – my pick being the Pizzini winery in Victoria, home to many of that country's best expressions of Italian varietals.

Here in New Zealand, sangiovese remains virtually unheard of – probably just as well, given that it has difficulty ripening here, to date.

Sangiovese is also known as sangioveto, brunello, prugnolo gentile and morellino, among other names.

Star sangiovese

2006 Cecchi Bonizio Sangiovese di Maremma

$19–20 ☆☆☆½

Made with grapes grown in Maremma in southern Tuscany, this bone-dry red is good with pasta. Fruit driven, spicy and slightly earthy, it is one of a new wave of southern Tuscan reds made from a single grape variety – in this case, sangiovese.

Glengarry stores in the North Island and specialist wine stores nationwide

2006 Pasqua Sangiovese $12–13 ☆☆☆½

It's the key grape in chianti, but sangiovese makes darned tasty stand-alone red wines too, such as this enormously good-value red. It's also available in a magnum (1500 ml – the equivalent of two bottles); both sizes are great value for money.

🛒 Glengarry stores in the North Island and specialist wine stores nationwide

Shiraz/syrah and blends

'Shi-rahz'/'See-raa'

Shiraz and syrah are two different names for the same grape variety and wine made from them. In Australia and South Africa it is usually shiraz; in France – the grape's home – it is syrah. As the sounds of the names imply, shiraz does tend to be a heavier, more gutsy red wine expression from this grape, while syrah is often softer, more spicy and peppery, and subtle. In New Zealand, most winemakers use the word syrah, and this country's climate tends to offer a more Rhône-like, less Australian interpretation of this grape.

Shiraz/syrah is among the greatest of all grape varieties – as are cabernet sauvignon, merlot, chardonnay, pinot noir, sauvignon blanc and riesling. And shiraz/syrah has the ability to evolve beautifully with age.

Despite the fact that many of the best wines made from this grape are French and labelled syrah, the word shiraz is gaining ground globally as the more favoured name – purely for marketing reasons.

Star shiraz

2005 Grant Burge Barossa Vines Shiraz

$19–20 ☆☆☆☆½

2005 Alliance McLaren Vale Shiraz $18–20 ☆☆☆½

This is a soft, jammy-tasting Australian red with smooth tannins and a medium-length finish. Good with great BBQ foods.

Specialist wine stores

2005 Ashwood Grove Victoria Shiraz $16–17 ☆☆☆½

To say that this wine is vibrant, fresh and positively packed with bright fruit flavours runs the risk of sounding repetitive but, hey, we're at the beginning of this chapter. This is great-value Australian shiraz, with all those qualities and more besides.

Specialist wine stores

2006 Beresford Beacon Hill South Eastern Australia Shiraz
$19–20 ☆☆☆☆ Screwcap

Talk about a surprisingly good drink. This southern Australian shiraz is explosively juicy – it positively brims over with rich, fruity aromas and flavours. It's spicy, weighty and has a long length of flavour with each mouthful. Needless to say, it's great value for money.

Specialist wine stores or contact Lace Fine Wine Merchants, phone (09) 828 4725 or email laceline@xtra.co.nz

2006 Beresford Highwood South Australia Shiraz
$15–16 ☆☆☆½ Screwcap

It's a tribute to Australia's great hot climate and very good winemaking that such a tasty, fresh, brightly fruited shiraz comes at this low price. It offers really good everyday drinking for those who like full-flavoured reds – and it has good length of flavour too, which is no mean feat at this price.

Specialist wine stores or contact Lace Fine Wine Merchants, phone (09) 828 4725 or email laceline@xtra.co.nz

2006 Beresford McLaren Vale Shiraz $25 ☆☆☆☆ Screwcap

This luscious big shiraz from pretty McLaren Vale in South Australia is great value for money and over-delivers on its bright fruit flavours, intense body and layers of taste. It has a long finish that adds to its appeal.

🛒 Specialist wine stores or contact Lace Fine Wine Merchants, phone (09) 828 4725 or email laceline@xtra.co.nz

2005 Brown Brothers Victoria Shiraz $18–19 ☆☆☆½ Screwcap

Like most reds in the growing Brown Brothers line-up, this Victorian shiraz is great value for money. It's also very young at the moment. Firm acids support rich, sweet fruit flavours, showing there is plenty of future potential. Should you be inclined to keep this wine a year or two, it will soften and improve in the bottle.

🛒 Widely available

2005 Climbing Shiraz $20–21 ☆☆☆☆ Screwcap

The evocative label on this bottle is just the cherry on the top of a really good, dry Australian shiraz. Yes, it's big and bold and gutsy as per classic Aussie shirazes, but it also has a dry finish and good balance. Needless to say, it's good value.

🛒 Specialist wine stores

2005 Cockatoo Ridge Shiraz $12–13 ☆☆☆½ Screwcap

It may be big on flavour, but this Aussie shiraz is low on price – and great value to boot. A blend of grapes grown in Barossa and McLaren Vale, it's rich and fruit driven, with long spicy flavours on the finish.

🛒 Widely available

2005 Commissioner's Block Shiraz $15–16 ☆☆☆½ Screwcap

This Australian shiraz brings an immediate softness to the palate – it's smooth, simple and off-dry with fruity sweetness. Good value for a reliable everyday red wine.

Widely available or www.robertsestatewines.com.au

2006 Cookoothama Shiraz $20–21 ☆☆☆☆

Like most Australian reds, this wine has a big hearty personality, lots of body and spicy aromas and taste. Like it a lot.

Glengarry stores in the North Island and specialist wine stores nationwide

2006 Corazón Syrah $24–25 ☆☆☆½

Corazón Wines is the brainchild of winemaker Shayne Cox, who is producing small quantities of this big, robust, single-vineyard syrah and other limited-edition wines at his winery on Henderson Valley Road, Auckland.

Specialist wine stores or www.corazonwines.co.nz

2005 Corbans Private Bin Hawke's Bay Syrah
$22–23 ☆☆☆½ Screwcap

New Zealand syrah is an up-and-coming grape in wine drinkers' minds more than in vineyards, where it still accounts for relatively little land area and grapes planted. This is an attractive, spicy wine – an interesting alternative for those who want to drink Kiwi reds that are full bodied. Good value.

Widely available

2006 Crossroads Hawke's Bay Syrah $19–20 ☆☆☆

Here's a fruity Hawke's Bay syrah (the same grape and wine as shiraz, just a different name). It's an earthy red that's slightly savoury tasting, with primary fruit flavours on the finish.

Specialist wine stores

2005 Deakin Estate Shiraz $15–16 ☆☆☆½ Screwcap

A solid, good-quality, everyday Australian red with rich, sweet, plummy flavours. Medium bodied and reliably fresh and flavoursome as an everyday wine.

Glengarry stores in the North Island and other specialist wine stores

2006 Deen De Bortoli Shiraz $20–21 ☆☆☆½

Here's a surprisingly intense-tasting red wine with loads of concentration, depth and length. It is a rewarding wine on its own, but far better served with your favourite savoury sausages or slow-roasted venison.

Glengarry stores in the North Island and specialist wine stores nationwide

2004 Duca di Castelmonte Syrah $19–20 ☆☆☆☆

Syrah is more famous as a Rhône Valley red, but it's also gaining ground – literally, in the vineyards – in Sicily. This is a lovely, soft-tannined, savoury-tasting red. It's great value for money.

Sovrano, Auckland, phone (09) 271 5969

2005 Element of Sandalford Shiraz Cabernet
$16–17 ☆☆☆½ Screwcap

Soft, fresh and good value, but a simple wine compared with other shirazes under the Sandalford label. Take this one to a BBQ.

Widely available

2005 Geoff Merrill Shiraz Grenache Mourvedre $23–24 ☆☆☆☆

Talk about an interesting blend of three hearty, distinctive grape varieties – all of which combine beautifully while retaining their own personalities in this big, characterful red.

Glengarry stores in the North Island and specialist wine stores nationwide

2006 Goldridge Estate Matakana Premium Reserve Syrah

$18–19 ☆☆☆½ Screwcap

Remember eating raspberry sherbert as a child? If not, a sip of this lovely, vibrant, raspberry-tasting syrah will instantly remind you. It's a light, honest style of Kiwi syrah, devoid of the usual over-oaking that most winemakers tend towards with syrah. Fresh, bright, easy to drink – great for a summer lunchtime or at a dinner party.

🛒 Specialist wine stores

Star shiraz

2005 Grant Burge Barossa Vines Shiraz

$19–20 ☆☆☆☆½ Screwcap

The only wonder is the price: how come this wine costs so little money when it tastes so extremely good? Well balanced, oozing ripe fruit flavours and lively acids to stretch it out to a lingering, memorable finish. Great value.

🛒 Liquor stores and specialist wine stores

2005 Hardys Nottage Hill South Australia Shiraz $10–12 ☆☆☆½

It's a cheapie, yes, but this is a reliably juicy, sweet but light-bodied South Australian shiraz.

🛒 Widely available

2006 Hardys Oomoo McLaren Vale Shiraz $18–19 ☆☆☆½

So, it's a big, juicy, gutsy Aussie shiraz – the likes of which are everywhere on wine shop shelves today – but this one over-delivers on rich plummy flavours and, importantly, on value for money.

🛒 Widely available

2005 Jacob's Creek Shiraz Cabernet $13–14 ☆☆☆½ Screwcap

Sure it's a big-brand red wine with tutti-frutti flavours, but this massively well-known Aussie red blend is also such easy, everyday drinking. Now that it sports a screwcap, it's hard to fault – good value.

🛒 Widely available

2006 Kingston Estate Shiraz $14–16 ☆☆☆

A simple, everyday Australian shiraz with sweet, plummy fruit flavours, but a slightly drying finish.

🛒 Widely available

2004 Knappstein Clare Valley Shiraz $19–20 ☆☆☆½ Screwcap

Bursting with the bright fruit flavours of South Australia – and good value to boot.

🛒 Liquor stores and specialist wine stores

2007 Lake Road Gisborne Syrah $19–20 ☆☆☆ Screwcap

This evocatively labelled syrah, made from Gisborne-grown grapes, is part of the growing stable of 'Boundary Road' wines – each comes from a different vineyard and region of New Zealand. This is a dense, dark red, with lots of earthy, savoury-driven flavours and a fruity hint on the finish.

🛒 Cafés, restaurants and specialist wine stores

2007 La Puerta Alta Syrah $20 ☆☆☆½

Undeniably South American in label design, wine flavour and robustness, this Argentinian syrah is as much about spicy peppery flavours as it is about upfront fruitiness. A good-value red.

🛒 Specialist wine stores or contact Bennett & Deller for stockists near you, phone (09) 378 9463

2006 Laroche Syrah $19–20 ☆☆☆½ Screwcap

Syrah is one of the fastest-growing red grapes in France, which is why this version comes from the south of France. It's soft, spicy and easy to drink, especially with slow-cooked meaty dishes.

Glengarry stores in the North Island and specialist wine stores nationwide

2005 Leasingham Clare Valley Magnus Shiraz
$24–25 ☆☆☆☆ Screwcap

This red is what good-value Aussie wines are all about – huge, rich, sweet berry flavours, medium body and a long finish. Medium bodied it may be, but this shiraz is very good value for everyday red-wine drinkers.

Widely available

2005 Milton Park Barossa Shiraz $16–17 ☆☆☆☆ Screwcap

Aside from the gorgeous label, this is a beautifully tasty, soft and fruity shiraz. Great value too.

Liquor stores and specialist wine stores

2006 Mission Hawke's Bay Mere Road Syrah
$18–20 ☆☆☆½ Screwcap

A step up in terms of firmness of tannins and youthfulness of flavour, this wine will take a little longer to settle and soften than its little sibling, below. Bigger, bolder, more peppery and more commanding.

Widely available

2006 Mission Hawke's Bay Syrah $16–18 ☆☆☆ Screwcap

Kiwi syrah is a peppery, fruity number, and this everyday version is also light, offering good BBQ drinking in summertime.

Widely available

2006 Mission Reserve Syrah $24–25 ☆☆☆

Peppery, fruity Hawke's Bay syrah that matches nicely with slow-cooked lamb shanks as a big winter comfort food.

🛒 Liquor stores and wine retailers

2005 Mitchelton Shiraz $18–20 ☆☆☆☆ Screwcap

Here's a big, spicy, plummy shiraz with more oomph than most everyday red wines. Good for dinner parties with savoury, gamey dishes or as a treat every day.

🛒 Liquor stores and specialist wine stores

2005 Moana Park Pascoe Series Syrah $17–18 ☆☆☆½ Screwcap

Syrah, the next big red hope according to some Kiwi winemakers, is big in name, though not yet in plantings in New Zealand. Most is grown in Hawke's Bay, where this robust, tight young red comes from. It's still youthful and, like many young reds under screwcap, really benefits from decanting – even into a large glass or a water jug, for an hour or two before serving.

🛒 Specialist wine stores or www.moanapark.co.nz

2006 Moana Park Syrah $16–18 ☆☆☆ Screwcap

Red-wine lovers looking for The Next Big Thing will enjoy this big, gutsy syrah from Hawke's Bay. It's heavily reliant on oak for much of its bold style and body, but there is nice, fresh fruitiness in here too.

🛒 Liquor stores and specialist wine stores

2007 Moana Park Vineyard Selection Syrah $18–20 ☆☆☆ Screwcap

A big, gutsy Hawke's Bay syrah, but still lighter in style than its Australian counterparts.

🛒 Liquor stores and specialist wine stores

2005 Mystery Creek Reserve Syrah $24–25 ☆☆☆ Screwcap

A little average, compared with the high quality of the white wines in the Mystery Creek line-up. Better than passable though, it's clean and fresh for an everyday plummy-tasting Kiwi syrah.

Specialist wine stores or www.mysterycreekwines.com

2005 Plantagenet Omrah Shiraz $19–20 ☆☆☆½ Screwcap

Thank goodness this wine is widely available, because it's stunning value for money – big and rich, but oddly enough also restrained for a shiraz at this price. Love the value it offers, which gives this wine the ability to work well midweek with pasta or pizza or at a posh weekend BBQ.

Widely available

2006 Preece Shiraz $19–20 ☆☆☆☆ Screwcap

An everyday shiraz that consistently offers very good value by over-delivering on flavour, body and length for the money you will spend on this wine.

Widely available

2006 Red Rock The Underarm Syrah $20 ☆☆☆☆ Screwcap

There's not a whiff of anything 'underarm' about this big, bold and squeaky clean Hawke's Bay red made from the syrah grape. There is lots of freshly cracked black pepper aromas, which are a hallmark of syrah. It's a fruit-driven red with ripe plum flavours, dense body and a spicy finish. Great value for money, and it shows how far Kiwi reds have come; this is very good.

Specialist wine stores or www.craggyrange.com

2003 Richmond Grove Limited Release Barossa Shiraz
$19–20 ☆☆☆½

Big, gutsy and apparently made in limited quantities (hence

'limited release' on the label), this is an intense, rich, fruity shiraz. Drink now or soon.

Widely available

2005 Rolling Shiraz $18–19 ☆☆☆☆ Screwcap

This is great value for money with surprisingly big, bold, rich plummy flavours and a weighty full-bodied style to boot. Too drinkable – and simply extraordinary value.

Specialist wine stores

2006 Saints Barossa Shiraz $16–18 ☆☆½ Screwcap

This wine is made from grapes grown in the Barossa Valley, Australia. It's a gutsy, fruit-driven red with rich plummy flavours and a spicy aroma coming through on the finish.

Widely available

2004 Sandalford Margaret River Shiraz $24–25 ☆☆☆½ Screwcap

Western Australian shiraz is a totally different creature to many others from Australia; more intense, with pure, plummy fruit flavours and a long finish. This is good value.

Specialist wine stores

2006 Selaks Favourite Hawke's Bay Syrah $20–21 ☆☆☆ Screwcap

Peppery, fruity Hawke's Bay syrah that is also light and simple – an everyday drinking style for an after-work glass or two.

Widely available

2005 Southbank Estate Hawke's Bay Syrah $24–25 ☆☆☆½

Upfront peppery aromas lead this wine into savoury flavours, which are best enjoyed with food – drink with a hearty winter meat dish.

Specialist wine stores

2006 Stone Paddock Pinot Noir $24–25 ☆☆☆½ Screwcap

Good but light . . . very light. This is a wine to start the evening with, not to finish with.

Widely available

2005 Tapestry McLaren Vale Shiraz $23–24 ☆☆☆½ Screwcap

No wonder red wine lovers enjoy Australian shiraz – it's wines like this that put them on that path in the first place. Big, bold and three years old, it's still fresh and has loads of life left, if you are inclined to buy a few bottles to cellar. Otherwise, enjoy now with great steak.

Widely available or www.tapestrywines.com.au

2006 Tapestry McLaren Vale Shiraz Viognier
$23–24 ☆☆☆½ Screwcap

The Australians pioneered varietally-labelled blending of shiraz with the white grape viognier – which is a traditional practice in France. The result is wines like this: an out-there, big fruit-bomb style with lovely fresh aromas and flavours – and good length.

Widely available or www.tapestrywines.com.au

2006 Taylors Clare Valley Shiraz $18–20 ☆☆☆½ Screwcap

Just to make sure all their bases are covered, the Taylor family now make several shirazes in this price range (see below for others). This is the most intensely dark, plummy, and richest in style with all the bells and whistles – but made entirely from shiraz. Good value.

Widely available

2005 Taylors Eighty Acres Shiraz Viognier
$19–20 ☆☆☆½ Screwcap

Not just a name but an actual vineyard, Eighty Acres was planted by Bill Taylor senior in 1969 in the Clare Valley, Australia. This new wine brand was launched late in 2007, and this wine is an appealing, lushly fruity, everyday red.

Widely available

2005 Taylors Promised Land Shiraz Cabernet

$14–16 ☆☆☆½ Screwcap

Here's a fantastic-tasting everyday red wine that offers good value for money. A blend of mostly shiraz, it has firm backbone, dark berry flavours and extra weight from the addition of cabernet.

Widely available

2006 Te Mania Nelson Syrah $23–25 ☆☆☆½

From a small, family-owned Nelson winery comes this super syrah – it's lively, fresh and rich with plum flavours. Great for everyday drinking or team it up with posh BBQ foods and game meats.

Specialist wine stores or email info@temaniawines.co.nz

2006 Thorn Clark Sandpiper Barossa Shiraz

$19–20 ☆☆☆☆ Screwcap

One word comes to mind after a sip of this rich, fruity shiraz has passed the lips: elegance. It's big and bold, yes, but has gorgeous freshness and firm acids that add length and elegance. Very good value at this price.

Widely available

2006 Three Stones South East Australia Shiraz

$18–20 ☆☆☆ Screwcap

A big, bold and fruity Aussie shiraz – this wine is all about sweet, plummy fruit flavours, and made in a drink-me-right-now style. Definitely an everyday number.

Widely available

2007 Timara Oak Aged Shiraz $12–13 ☆☆☆ Screwcap

It may be oak-aged but this is a light red with lots of spicy flavours and soft red fruitiness. Definitely an everyday number.

Widely available

2006 Trinity Hill Hawke's Bay Shiraz $20 ☆☆☆½ Screwcap

Just as you'd expect from Hawke's Bay winemakers John Hancock and Warren Gibson – bright, fresh and highly drinkable, with intense, ripe plum flavours. Great everyday wine, good for a BBQ, or decant it and this will stand up to savoury winter dishes at a dinner party.

Widely available at wine stores and liquor stores nationwide or email enquiries@trinityhill.com

2006 Vidal Hawke's Bay Syrah $24–25 ☆☆☆½ Screwcap

Lovely, big, black peppery Hawke's Bay red made from syrah, which is growing massively internationally and slowly in New Zealand's vineyards (though strongly in our mindsets). Good value for a robust, wintery, full-bodied local red.

Widely available

2006 Villa Maria Hawke's Bay Syrah $22–23 ☆☆☆ Screwcap

Dark black peppery and deep spicy flavours combine with soft plum tastes in this red to show what New Zealand syrah is all about.

Widely available

2005 Wirra Wirra Scrubby Rise Shiraz Cabernet Sauvignon Petit Verdot $19–20 ☆☆☆☆ Screwcap

Here's what Australian reds do best at this price – when led by shiraz as the dominant red grape in the blend. Ripe and juicy, this is a wine that just seems to cry 'drink me round the fire or BBQ'.

Liquor stores and specialist wine stores or www.wirrawirra.com

2005 Wyndham Estate Bin 555 Shiraz $16–17 ☆☆☆½ Screwcap

Surprise you it may, but this well-known and low-priced shiraz is simply great everyday drinking. A shiraz lover or not, you'll enjoy its clean, fresh, fruity flavours that are nicely balanced in an easy-to-drink, light to medium-bodied package.

🛒 Widely available

2004 Wyndham Estate George Wyndham Shiraz $22–23 ☆☆☆☆

This shiraz is from the historic Wyndham Estate winery in the Hunter Valley, Australia, and is fantastic value for money. Four years old now, it still has lots of life left in it (if you're inclined to keep it any longer), otherwise enjoy with braised beef.

🛒 Widely available

2006 Zilzie Selection 23 Shiraz $15–16 ☆☆☆½ Screwcap

Talk about a big, robust Aussie shiraz . . . this is firm and young still, even at two years old. Good for drinking with slow-roasted meat dishes in midwinter or around a fire on a cold night.

🛒 Specialist wine stores

2005 Zilzie Shiraz $18–19 ☆☆☆½

At three years old, this shiraz is ready to be enjoyed now – preferably with gamey flavours such as venison sausages on the BBQ. It's spicy and slightly earthy.

🛒 Specialist wine stores

Tempranillo

'Temp-ran-ee-oh'

Tempranillo is one of the exciting grapes on the planet right now, due to Spain's rise and rise in the wine world. The best description comes from Jancis Robinson, a Master of Wine, who describes it as the grape that puts the spine into Spanish reds. The word 'temprano' means 'early' in Spanish, and tempranillo is an early-ripening grape variety (up to two weeks earlier than garnacha, Spain's biggest red). There is a little tempranillo grown in other countries, most notably in southern France and parts of Australia, with smatterings elsewhere (including Hawke's Bay, New Zealand), but mostly this is a Spanish grape all the way.

2004 Torres Coronas Tempranillo $18–20 ☆☆☆½

This is one of the best-known Spanish wine brands in New Zealand – and great value too. Tempranillo is such a delicious grape and wine; perfect for winter with its flavours of rich, stewed fruit and a savoury, lingering finish.

Liquor stores and specialist wine stores

2004 Torres Coronas Tempranillo Cabernet $20–21 ☆☆☆½

This is pure heartland Spain in a bottle – with a modern twist. There are two grapes in this wine: the traditional Spanish tempranillo with French cabernet sauvignon. Blended together they make a rich, savoury treat that tastes great with slow-cooked roast lamb.

Specialist wine stores

Valpolicella

'Val-pol-ee-chell-a'

There may only be a few wines featured here, but this is a growing market; light, lush reds with quirky, interesting, savoury flavours. In many ways, valpolicella could be said to be Italy's answer to beaujolais, with its soft tannins, vibrant acids and light fruit weight making an easy-to-like, drink-me-now red wine style. Valpolicella is made from corvine, rondinella and molinara grapes in the Veneto region of Italy.

Star valpolicella

2006 Bolla Valpolicella Classico $18–19 ☆☆☆½

The newest and the best valpolicella in New Zealand under $25 right now. Savoury, soft, light and tasty. Great value.

Glengarry stores in the North Island and specialist wine stores nationwide

2005 Cecilia Beretta Valpolicella Superiore $18–19 ☆☆☆

This is a light, fresh-tasting Italian red – which tastes better with foods than without; drink with your favourite nibbles.

Glengarry stores in the North Island and specialist wine stores nationwide

2006 Pasqua Valpolicella $16–17 ☆☆☆

Is it just this vintage, or has this wine become a lighter version of its former self? Soft, simple and lightly fruity, this is definitely an everyday red to enjoy early in the evening.

Glengarry stores in the North Island and specialist wine stores nationwide

Zinfandel

'Zin-fan-del'

California's unique offering to the world of wine was for a long time thought to be either a mutation or a clonal variation of the Italian grape primitivo. In fact, zinfandel's parentage is far more complicated and originates from Croatia. This is a black-skinned, intensely sweet and fruity-tasting grape that makes wines with high alcohol levels. If North American culture is best known for its 'big is better' philosophy, then zinfandel fits in perfectly. It is also easily likeable, though grown in few other places, including Chile and Australia.

2005 Ravenswood Vintners Blend California Zinfandel

$19–20 ☆☆☆

For a wine that's three years old, made from an almost unheard-of grape variety (zinfandel) and from North America, this is worth drinking for quirk value alone. It's also an intense, rewarding red to welcome in the winter months.

🛒 Specialist wine stores and from Wine Direct, Newmarket, Auckland, in store or www.winedirect.co.nz

Bubbles

Star bubbly

Lindauer Special Reserve 2004

$24–25 ☆☆☆☆

Star bubbly under $10

Bernadino Spumante

$8–9 ☆☆☆½

Star prosecco

Bolla Prosecco NV

$22–23 ☆☆☆☆

Star bubbly under $10

Bernadino Spumante

$8–9 ☆☆☆½

If you haven't tried this lovely, aromatic, New Zealand sparkling bubbly for a while, then it's high time you reacquainted yourself with its transparent fruity style. It's a consistently honest, fruity little number that's easy to drink chilled in summer in a jug with ice and mint. Great value too.

Widely available

Star prosecco

Bolla Prosecco NV

$22–23 ☆☆☆☆

This vibrant, zingy Italian prosecco has a great taste and offers great value for money. As its price implies, this wine is definitely a cut above the everyday drinking band, but it's so tasty that it's tempting to have plenty on hand simply to be able to enjoy a glass once a day – after work, of course. Lovely fresh, clean and nutty flavours.

🛒 Glengarry stores in the North Island and specialist wine stores nationwide

Carpene Malvolti Brut Prosecco NV $23–24 ☆☆☆☆

Prosecco is the drier of northern Italy's bubbly styles and this one is clean and fresh – the perfect bubbles to kick-start an evening. Serve chilled with good friends and enjoy.

🛒 Foodtown and Woolworths supermarkets, or La Barrique, Auckland, phone (09) 638 5000 or 524 6666

Carpene Malvolti Rosé NV $23–24 ☆☆☆½

Pink wine is one of the most popular things right now all over the world – sans or avec bubbles. This deep-pink Italian bubbly is light, fresh and just off-dry.

🛒 Foodtown and Woolworths supermarkets, or La Barrique, Auckland, phone (09) 638 5000 or 524 6666

Cockatoo Ridge NV Brut $12–13 ☆☆☆

It's bubbles like these that bring good-quality sparkling wine to everybody at an affordable price – that said, this is an entry-level bubbly for everyday or BBQ enjoyment.

🛒 Widely available

Commissioner's Block Brut Cuvée $15–16 ☆☆☆

This is a reliably good everyday Australian bubbles. Good value for a BBQ.

Widely available

Deakin Brut NV $17–18 ☆☆☆

This is a lively, fresh, everyday bubbles with lots of vibrancy and bright fruit flavours. Very 'New World' in style, with a reliable consistency, making it good value.

Glengarry stores in the North Island and specialist wine stores nationwide

Jacob's Creek Chardonnay Pinot Noir Brut Cuvée $10–12 ☆☆☆

Good-value everyday bubbles don't get better than this at under $15. It's a classic 'champagne blend' of chardonnay with pinot noir, albeit in a very fruity style (compared with the world of champagne). Chill – the wine and yourself – and enjoy.

Widely available

Jacob's Creek Sparkling Rosé $10–12 ☆☆☆½

This light-pink Australian rosé is bottle fermented and good value for an off-dry everyday celebration – or even just everyday enjoyment. Just be sure to chill it down and enjoy with salted nuts and nibbles.

Widely available

2007 JC Le Roux Naturally Delicate Red $15–16 ☆☆☆

Despite its slightly odd name, this light, fizzy red is a good introduction to wine – so long as it's served chilled.

Liquor stores and selected specialist wine stores or contact Vintage Wines, phone (09) 480 0789

2007 JC Le Roux Naturally Lively White $15–16 ☆☆☆

A simple, light, fizzy white from South Africa. Serve chilled during the day – preferably outside at the beach or park – with nibbles.

Liquor stores and selected specialist wine stores or contact Vintage Wines, phone (09) 480 0789

2007 JC Le Roux Sauvignon Blanc $15–16 ☆☆☆

In South Africa, a country whose wine industry is awash with sauvignon blanc, you might think it a little odd to encounter one with bubbles. Strange or not, this unlikely sparkling sauvignon is a refreshing bubbly with a dry-ish finish. Be sure to serve chilled and drink with food – fresh seafood preferably.

Liquor stores and selected specialist wine stores or contact Vintage Wines, phone (09) 480 0789

Lindauer Brut $16–17 ☆☆☆☆

To make a bottle-fermented bubbly at this price is no mean feat; it says a lot about the economies of scale of a large wine company and its ability to turn out consistent everyday quality. This bubbles is full bodied mid-palate and has a weighty, slightly lingering finish.

Widely available

Lindauer Cuvée Riche $14–16 ☆☆☆

Good-quality new addition to the globally famous Lindauer range; it is light and simple and unashamedly sweet. Drink it with the Christmas trifle and add some to the dessert for good measure.

Widely available

Lindauer Sec $16–17 ☆☆☆½

This is incredible value for money, not least because the price stays the same year after year. Its off-dry style gives this wine huge appeal and it finishes on a lingering, crisp, chardonnay-tasting flavour.

Widely available

Lindauer Special Reserve $16–17 ☆☆☆☆

This is fantastic value for money and, as last year, it is one of the best, most champagne-like bottle of bubbles tried for the guide this year, with its yeasty flavours and long finish.

Widely available

Star bubbly

Lindauer Special Reserve 2004

$24–25 ☆☆☆☆

A front-runner for anybody looking for decent bubbles under $25; this is top notch in quality and in the value for money that it delivers. Rounded and creamy, and although off-dry, it is still sensationally good.

Widely available

Lindauer Special Reserve Blanc de Blancs $16–17 ☆☆☆☆

As always, a delicious bubbly for chardonnay fans, with instantly recognisable and easy-to-like, fruit-upfront flavours. It is great value.

Widely available

Preece Mitchelton Sparkling $18–20 ☆☆☆½

This is an everyday sparkling wine with crisp acids, rounded full body and a barely noticeable just off-dry style, which adds subtle but powerful appeal. Very good value.

Widely available

Riccadonna Asti $16–18 ☆☆☆½

Delicious chilled and served with fresh mint and wedges of lime, which tame down the overt aromatic profile of this intensely aromatic, sweet bubbly. A great lunchtime wine.

Widely available

Riccadonna Ruby $16–18 ☆☆☆½

Never underestimate the power of a good moscato; this pink sweetie is lovely served chilled in the middle of the day – or ice cold on your favourite beach.

Widely available

Torralta Prosecco $20–22 ☆☆☆

Its light, fresh aromatic style, lowish alcohol content of 11 per cent and fresh style make this Italian bubbles a delicious anytime wine, served lightly chilled, of course.

Specialist wine stores

Trilogy Pinot Noir Chardonnay Pinot Meunier $14–16 ☆☆☆

This is always one of the best-value bubbles under $20 each year. Made from the three classic champagne grapes: pinot noir, chardonnay and pinot meunier – hence the name. This is dry-ish, light and fresh, making it a great everyday bubbles style.

Specialist wine stores

Twin Islands Brut NV $15–16 ☆☆☆☆

It's rare to find such quality in bubbles that still leave you spare change from a $20 note. This one is not only méthode traditionelle (for which, read its secondary fermentation took place in the bottle), but it is also made from champagne's two main grape varieties – pinot noir and chardonnay – which accounts for its full mouthfeel and citrusy finish.

Widely available

Verde Chardonnay Pinot Noir $17–18 ☆☆☆½

This is a light and refreshingly bone-dry bubbly made from champagne grapes, chardonnay and pinot noir. It's always been great value for money and this year it is again.

Widely available

Wyndham Estate Sparkling Shiraz NV $16–17 ☆☆☆½

Award winning or not, this shiraz with bubbles is a refreshingly new take on bubbly for a hot day. Treat it exactly as you would any sparkling wine and chill it right down before enjoying with food in the sunshine – it's a good match for tasty cheese, great parmigiana, manchego or your favourite cheese.

Widely available

Dessert wines

Star dessert wine

2006 Gran Feudo Blanco Dulce de Moscatel

$24–25 ☆☆☆☆½

2007 Alpha Domus The Pilot Leonarda Late Harvest Semillon
$19–20 ☆☆☆☆ Screwcap

It's not that often you see a dessert wine made from semillon in New Zealand. This is a deliciously honey-tasting pudding wine – not cloying, but nicely balanced. Good value, too.

🛒 Specialist wine stores or www.alphadomus.co.nz

2007 Brown Brothers Special Late Harvested Orange Muscat & Flora $14–15 ☆☆☆½ Screwcap

Haven't heard of 'orange muscat and flora'? No worries – just get yourself a bottle of this to enjoy chilled on Christmas morning with panettone – Italian Christmas cake. Its delicious aromatics will wow you first thing in the day.

🛒 Widely available or email djmchenry@brownbrothers.com.au

2007 Forrest Estate Late Harvest Marlborough Gewürztraminer
$18–20 ☆☆☆☆ Screwcap

Dessert gewürztraminers are hardly a dime a dozen, in any winemaking country. Related mostly to rarity status or maiden aunts, gewürztraminer sometimes seems destined for complete obscurity, but try an unctuous, expressively floral wine like this and you'll soon wonder why. Chill and drink with lemon desserts or on its own.

Widely available or www.forrestwines.co.nz

Garofoli Dorato Vino Dolce $23–24 ☆☆☆☆

Southern Italian dessert wines are thin on the ground in New Zealand, but this lovely fresh one breaks new ground for Kiwi palates. Rather than being 'sticky', this is a nicely balanced, lusciously aromatic Italian dessert wine – served lightly chilled, it tastes refreshing to finish a meal with.

Sovrano, Auckland, phone (09) 271 5969

Star dessert wine

2006 Gran Feudo Blanco Dulce de Moscatel

$24–25 ☆☆☆☆½

What better way to refresh your tastebuds than with this gorgeously aromatic Spanish moscatel (that's muscat to us Kiwis). It's a fantastically unadulterated version of one of the most underappreciated white grapes in the world – muscat. Intense in aromatics and taste, with a light body and long finish, this is great value.

Fine Wine Delivery Company in Auckland and other specialist wine stores, or contact Bennett & Deller Wine Merchants, phone (09) 378 9463

2006 Grove Mill Marlborough Late Harvest Gewürztraminer

$18–20 ☆☆☆☆ Screwcap

Ever tasted a dessert gewürztraminer before? It's a relatively unusual grape to make pudding wine from – in this country at least – but it works a treat. The grape's natural intense aromatics easily lend themselves to the unctuous, full-bodied sweetness here. This is great value for money too.

Specialist wine stores

2004 Montana Late Harvest $16–17 ☆☆☆½ Screwcap

Great-value entry-level 'late harvest' (which means that the grapes were picked late) pudding wine. Drink it with your favourite version of lemon meringue pie and enjoy the citrusy and honeyed unctuousness of the wine with the food, or enjoy on its own – either way, chill it.

Widely available

2007 Sileni Late Harvest Hawke's Bay Semillon
$20–21 ☆☆☆½ Screwcap

This lovely Hawke's Bay semillon is lighter in style than many Kiwi pudding wines – I like it precisely because of those fresh, clean flavours and lighter-than-usual texture. It has nuances of liquid honey and good balance. Great value too.

Widely available

2006 Stone Paddock Isabella Late Harvest Semillon
$21–23 ☆☆☆½ Screwcap

Its makers describe this wine as tasting of orange peel, prune and floral aromas, which I entirely agree with. It has impressive intensity of flavour and a spicy finish. Lovely stuff.

Specialist wine stores or www.paritua.com

2007 Te Mania Nelson Ice Wine $21–22 ☆☆☆½ Screwcap

There is no clue as to which grapes are in this 'ice wine', which pays homage to the rare world of ice wines – those that are made from grapes harvested in temperatures so cold that they are actually frozen on the vines. Nelson is not quite that cold, so this is a sweet pudding wine, made to be served chilled and with either a citrusy dessert or a slightly salty, aged cheese.

🛒 Specialist wine stores

2006 Valli Vin Santo Pinot Gris $24–25 ☆☆☆ Screwcap

A Tuscan-inspired dessert wine made by Grant Taylor, whose great-grandfather Guiseppe Valli – an Italian immigrant to New Zealand – made wine in Italy. This 'vin santo' (holy wine) is made, rather unusually, from pinot gris grown in Central Otago. Interesting savoury and sweet flavours intermingle here. Drink with hard, crumbly cheese.

🛒 Specialist wine stores or www.valliwine.com

2006 Waimea Late Harvest Nelson Riesling

$18–20 ☆☆☆½ Screwcap

Riesling retains its luscious lime, lemon and apple flavours – even when made into a sweet wine such as this one. Team this up with lemon tart, both served lightly chilled, and you'll love it.

🛒 Specialist wine stores or www.waimeaestates.co.nz

Fortified wines

These wines are all from Australia and New Zealand and made in the mould of port, but since they are not made in Portugal they can only be called fortified wines – only fortified wines made in Portugal can officially lay claim to the name port.

Morris Liqueur Tawny Port $18–20 ☆☆☆½

A light port with spicy, cedary tastes. Good value for basic port requirements – not remarkable, but still very smooth and drinkable, especially with a tasty cheddar.

Specialist wine stores

Morris Liqueur Tokay $19–20 ☆☆☆

Mellow, spicy, sweet wine without the cloying factor, but offering up loads of interesting tastes – perfect with cakey desserts with unctuous, even chocolatey, sauces rather than cheeses. Love the price and the wine.

Specialist wine stores

Star fortified wine

Orlando Liqueur Port

$18–20 ☆☆☆½

Lovely, mellow, spicy-tasting Australian port with smooth body and treacly flavours. Lovely stuff, even served lightly chilled; drink with aged cheddar.

Specialist wine stores

Sherries

Just as port can only come from Portugal, true sherry can only come from Spain – in particular, the south of Spain. And one of the defining characteristics of sherry is its affordability, even for the most complex and interesting versions, as these wines attest to.

Star sherry

Sandeman Dry Sec Sherry

$18–20 ☆☆☆½

This is a manzanilla-style fino sherry, salty and fresh, with lovely bone-dry flavours and qualities – fantastic. The best of this range by a long shot and great served with green olives.

Specialist wine stores

Sandeman Medium Dry Sherry $18–20 ☆☆☆

A sweeter-than-usual amontillado style with lovely true-to-type salty flavours and a rich, golden-treacle-tasting finish. This is a lovely wine and great value at this under-$20 price. Serve your favourite paté with a glass of this wine chilled before dinner.

Specialist wine stores

A–Z of wines under three stars

2006 Bach 22 Merlot $12–14 ☆☆½ Screwcap

2006 Bensen Block Hawke's Bay Cabernet Merlot
$16–18 ☆☆½ Screwcap

2006 Bolla Pinot Grigio $16–18 ☆☆½

2006 Bolla Sangiovese Di Romagna $17–18 ☆☆½

2006 Cecchi Chianti DOCG $21–22 ☆☆½

2004 Crossroads Destination Series Merlot Cabernet Sauvignon
$19–20 ☆☆ Screwcap

2006 Danzante Pinot Grigio $19–20 ☆☆½

2004 Distant Land Hawke's Bay Chardonnay $18–20 ☆☆ Screwcap

2007 Drostdy-Hof Cape Red $12–13 ☆½

2007 Huntaway Reserve Pinot Gris $18–20 ☆☆½ Screwcap

2007 Kaikoura Marlborough Unoaked Chardonnay
$19–20 ☆☆½ Screwcap

2005 Kingston Estate Cabernet Sauvignon $16–18 ☆☆

2006 Kingston Estate Merlot $16–18 ☆☆

2005 Kono Gisborne Merlot $18–20 ☆☆ Screwcap

Lake Chalice Cracklin' Rosie Marlborough Pinot Rosé
$18–20 ☆☆½

2007 Lake Chalice Merlot $20–21 ☆☆½ Screwcap

2007 Lawson's Dry Hills Pinot Gris $23–24 ☆☆½ Screwcap

2005 Main Divide Merlot Cabernet $19–20 ☆☆½ Screwcap

2006 Moana Park Vineyard Tribute Merlot $17–18 ☆☆½

Monkey Bay Cabernet Merlot $10–12 ☆☆ Screwcap

Monkey Bay Merlot $10–12 ☆☆ Screwcap

2006 Montana Hawke's Bay Merlot Cabernet Sauvignon
$14–16 ☆☆½ Screwcap

2007 Montana North Island Pinot Gris $14–15 ☆☆ Screwcap

2006 Mud House Swan Marlborough Merlot $18–19 ☆☆ Screwcap

2007 Nobilo East Coast Pinot Gris $14–16 ☆☆ Screwcap

2006 Pasqua La Collezioni Merlot $12–13 ☆☆

2007 Saints Gisborne Pinot Gris $17–18 ☆☆½ Screwcap

2007 Selaks Cabernet Sauvignon $14–16 ☆☆ Screwcap

2007 Selaks Favourite Gisborne Viognier $14–16 ☆☆½ Screwcap

2006 Selaks Favourite Hawke's Bay Merlot Cabernet
$14–16 ☆☆ Screwcap

2007 Southbank Estate East Coast Pinot Gris $20–21 ☆☆ Screwcap

2007 Southbank Estate Hawke's Bay Merlot
$20–21 ☆☆½ Screwcap

2007 Southbank Estate Hawke's Bay Merlot Cabernet
$20–21 ☆☆½ Screwcap

2006 Te Mania Three Brothers Merlot Malbec Cabernet
$18–20 ☆☆½

2006 Timara Oak Aged Cabernet Merlot $14–16 ☆☆½ Screwcap

2007 Trapiche Mendoza Pinot Noir $14–16 ☆☆½

2007 Zilzie Pinot Grigio $18–19 ☆☆ Screwcap